One Pound, Twelve Ounces

One Pound, Twelve Ounces

A Preemie Mother's Story of
Loss, Hope, and Triumph

Melissa Harris

[swp]

SHE WRITES PRESS

Published 2021

Printed in the United States of America

Print ISBN: 978-1-64742-213-4
E-ISBN: 978-1-64742-214-1
Library of Congress Control Number: 2021912122

For information, address:
She Writes Press
1569 Solano Ave #546
Berkeley, CA 94707

She Writes Press is a division of SparkPoint Studio, LLC.

This book is dedicated to the staff
of Alta Bates hospital,
heroes in surgical masks.

My mom,
whose love and support are missed every day.

And to Sam and Irene,
you two are my everything.

Prologue

2010

I had a plan.

It seemed like such a simple plan.

Two kids, two years apart—and before I was thirty-five.

My husband, Peter, and I were in agreement. He was an only child, and my brother and I were four and a half years apart. Growing up, I always wished we had been closer in age.

We managed to accomplish the first part of the plan easily. Within two months of deciding we were ready to have a child, I was pregnant with Irene. Despite being uncomfortable and suffering from pretty bad acid reflux, my pregnancy was unremarkable. It wasn't until the end when Irene refused to come out and I was induced two and a half weeks after my due date that I felt like I understood why some people hated being pregnant.

It was the second child who was proving to be difficult. For two years, I kept adjusting the plan until finally, it looked like everything was coming together. I was pregnant and heading toward my last trimester.

So how the hell did I end up in Labor & Delivery contracting every two minutes with my head below my feet at just twenty-three weeks and two days pregnant?

Part One

Infertility, Miscarriages, and Premature Birth

Chapter 1

2010

Trendelenburg. That is the technical name for the position I was in. The head of my hospital bed was tilted downward at a thirty-degree angle. The first few moments were so surreal, I felt like I could slide off the end of the bed at any moment. Then, I felt all of the blood in my body rush to my head, and the room began to spin.

I was contracting every two minutes, and the gestational sac was partially out of my uterus. The idea behind Trendelenburg is to use gravity to move the gestational sac back where it belongs. And, until the sac was back inside the uterus, I was told not to move, as any movement could cause the sac to rupture.

On top of the gravity-defying position I was in, my body was being pumped full of the contraction-stopping drug magnesium sulfate. In addition to helping stop contractions, magnesium sulfate also causes headaches and body sweats.

It seemed like hours before a doctor came in to talk to me. Up until then, I knew things were bad, but I didn't understand how bad.

"At this point, I can't tell you if we will be successful in stopping the progression of your labor," the obstetrician on call said quietly.

"What happens if we can't stop it?" Peter asked timidly.

"Unfortunately, it is too early for your baby to be born and survive," the doctor replied.

That was it for me. I was no longer able to focus on what was being said or the people around me. I was deep in my own head, trying to figure out what I had done wrong and doing my best to push down the primal scream that was building up inside of me. I wanted to unleash it all. Scream. Cry. Lash out. But the only thing I was able to do was weep—carefully.

I understood it was too early to have the baby. At the time, I knew most doctors consider twenty-four weeks to be the earliest point of viability. I was still a few days shy of that mark.

I had worked so hard to become pregnant. I had been through so much. Ever since I peed on the stick and it came back positive, I had fallen in love with the baby growing inside of me. I had so much hope wrapped up in this little one that the thought of losing him or her was more than I could bear.

Chapter 2

2008

The first miscarriage happened so early in the pregnancy, I never really even felt pregnant. It seemed like the moment Peter and I decided it was time to work on baby number two, we were pregnant. As easy as it was to get pregnant, it turned out it was just as easy to lose the baby.

After that miscarriage, getting pregnant again became difficult. We struggled mightily and months passed without a positive result. We finally got to the point where my obstetrician felt we needed to see a fertility specialist, Dr. Chetkowski.

For Peter, a visit to the fertility doctor meant a quick sperm count and motility check (he passed with flying colors). For me, it was a much more involved process. I had to have my entire reproductive system mapped through a combination of MRIs, X-rays, and blood tests. The results were disheartening.

It turned out that I was a walking reproductive nightmare. I didn't ovulate every cycle; my uterus is severely tilted, making it hard for the sperm to get where it needs to go; my cervix doesn't close all the way, making it hard to trap the sperm in the uterus so they can get to the egg; and, most troubling, I had a bicornuate uterus with a septum creating two distinct chambers.

Chapter 3

2010

The first night in Labor & Delivery was pretty much a blur. I know my mom and Peter spent the night on the couch in my room, curled up next to each other, snoring. I know my night nurse, Nora, sat next to my bed holding my hand all night and telling me to keep breathing and to take it easy. I know my head was on fire from the magnesium sulfate. I know my contractions became stronger and I was given a button to push each time I felt one (still every two minutes). I know I cried, all night long.

Once morning came, the doctors added a new drug to my IV, Procardia, in the hopes that it would help slow my contractions (it did). Then an ultrasound machine was wheeled into my room to see whether being in Trendelenburg had helped get the sac back where it belonged (it hadn't). Worse than that, the ultrasound now showed that I was dilated to eight centimeters, just two centimeters shy of where you need to be for delivery.

Despite the contractions being slower, they had grown in intensity. I felt each and every one of them. They were so strong, I had to ask for something to help dull the pain.

Not long after getting the pain killer, we were visited by the perinatologist on call. I will refer to him as Dr. Doom. He was the most negative man I had ever met.

"So, after looking at the ultrasound, and the frequency of your contractions, I believe this is a doomed pregnancy, and you should stop treatment and let it go," Dr. Doom said in a monotonous, emotionless tone.

"Let it go? What the hell does that mean?" I asked, my attention fully on the doctor.

"Your body is trying to terminate the pregnancy. I am suggesting you stop all treatment and let that happen," he replied.

I had been told to stay calm, and this man was doing his best to get me to lose my shit.

"I am sure you will be delivering by this evening, and, as the fetus is not even twenty-four weeks, it is not viable and will not survive," Dr. Doom added.

"We will not be making any decisions until we talk with Dr. Kasahara," Peter hissed through his clenched teeth.

Dr. Kasahara, our high-risk obstetrician, was already on her way to the hospital. We wanted to hear her opinion before we made any decisions.

"We need some time to process all of this. Can you give us some space?" This was Peter's gentle way of telling Dr. Doom to get lost before he upset me further, or my mother unleashed her anger on him. The doctor left, but not before telling us again how dire our situation was and how we needed to make some difficult decisions—and fast.

Chapter 4

2008

After getting the results of my fertility testing, I was sure that Irene was going to be an only child. When the doctor outlined a plan of attack, I was shocked and pleasantly surprised.

The most important issue to resolve was my bicornuate uterus. The doctor needed to remove the septum that was causing the division. Apparently one of my two chambers was too small for a baby to grow in, so if the egg decided to implant on the wrong side, I was guaranteed to miscarry.

Septum removal is an outpatient surgical procedure where the doctor inserts a camera and other medical devices through the cervix into the uterus while the patient is under twilight sedation. Think of it as a standard gynecological exam on steroids—with an assist from some good knockout drugs. Yes, it is as pleasant as it sounds!

Each time the doctor went in, he ran into something that made it hard to remove the full septum. It took six tries to finally create one uniform uterine chamber.

Unfortunately, each surgery meant a delay of two months in even trying to get pregnant as it took that long for the cervix to recover and the anesthesia drugs to fully clear my system.

In addition to removing the septum, I was going to take a

fertility drug that was supposed to stimulate one egg follicle to be released every cycle. Deciding to leave nothing to chance, I opted to move forward with an IUI (intrauterine insemination), or as I like to call it, the turkey baster method.

Five weeks after the first IUI, I was late. I had been charting my period for a while, so I knew exactly when it was due. I didn't want to say anything for fear of jinxing things. I went out and got a home pregnancy kit. The best time to take one of those tests is first thing in the morning, so I hid the box in the bathroom and went to bed. I must have woken up every hour that night. Finally, at 4 a.m., I broke down and took the test. Within three minutes of peeing on the stick, the results were in, and they were inconclusive.

Frustrated, I went out to our bedroom and shook Peter awake.

"I peed on a stick," I said.

"OK. What time is it?"

"It's four a.m. But I peed on a stick."

Slowly sitting up, Peter looked at me a little angry and confused.

"Why are you telling me this at four a.m.?" he asked.

"Because, I'm late."

"How late?" Peter was now fully awake and aware of what we were talking about.

"Maybe a week. The test was . . . confusing."

"Bring it here. Let me look."

I went and got the test to show Peter. He looked at it long and hard and said, "What the hell does that mean?"

I was comforted that the results confused him as well. We decided to wait until a more reasonable hour to take the test again. At 8 a.m., I peed on another stick, and this one was much clearer. I was pregnant. As soon as the doctor's office opened, I called to make an appointment. I wanted this result confirmed by a doctor.

Two days later I got my blood drawn, and the following day I went in to see my doctor. He had the results of the blood work and confirmed that I was pregnant.

Holy shit, I was pregnant!

Chapter 5

2010

D r. Kasahara arrived soon after Dr. Doom's departure. Without sugarcoating our critical situation, Dr. Kasahara presented us with a few options.

"You understand that as of today, your baby would not survive if born?" Dr. Kasahara asked.

I was still three days shy of that magic viability mark—twenty-four weeks. If a baby is born before the twenty-four-week mark, the survival chances are very slim, and survival without major medical issues even slimmer. Making things a bit more complicated was the fact that we didn't know if we were having a boy or a girl. The statistics for girls are more encouraging than the statistics for boys. Even so, I was determined not to know the sex of this baby. If we had a boy, I wanted to name him after my uncle Sam, who had been killed in 2004 when he was hit by a car while out on a bike ride. The thought of losing another Sam seemed too overwhelming, so not knowing the sex of this baby became crucial for me. I just didn't want to know that I had a baby boy inside of me that might not make it.

"I know I have to hold on for three days—right?" I mumbled, slowly joining the conversation from my drug-induced haze.

"That's right, Melissa. You need to get to twenty-four weeks before we can even begin to talk about viability."

Dr. Kasahara's tone was so calm and caring. I felt safe in her words. If she told me it was hopeless, I would believe her. But here she was, offering hope.

"Do you think there is any way to save this pregnancy?" Peter asked.

"I can't give you any guarantees, but I have seen it happen," Dr. Kasahara replied. "If you want to try, we need Melissa to hang on for three more days. At that point, our options will be different."

"I can do this. I can hold on. I can lie here. I can stay calm. Please, give me a chance to save this baby!" I pleaded with Dr. Kasahara, and also with Peter. He was the one who was coherent. I needed him to advocate for me and our child with the doctors and nurses.

"I believe you, Melissa," Dr. Kasahara said. "So, now comes some tough decisions. If your baby is born before twenty-four weeks, the survival outcomes are not good. Do you want us to resuscitate anyway?"

Peter looked at me. I closed my eyes and shook my head slowly.

"No. If the baby is born before twenty-four weeks, we do not want extraordinary measures taken," Peter answered for the two of us.

"What do you want to do if Melissa's life is in danger before twenty-four weeks?" Dr. Kasahara asked in her calmest voice.

"Melissa's health comes first." Peter did not look to me for this answer. He was right, of course.

"OK. We will keep all the medications going with the hope of getting you across the twenty-four-week mark. However, if Melissa's condition changes, we are all in agreement that we will deliver and not resuscitate. And, if delivery means a C-section, you are both authorizing that?"

"Yes," Peter answered. He was handed a consent form to sign. They wanted the consent signed now, in case my situation deteriorated quickly.

"Once we are across that twenty-four-week mark, I will come back and we will talk through the next decisions you will need to make. I would encourage you to learn the sex of the baby. Outcomes are very different for boys than they are for girls."

"We agreed not to find out. Can you put the gender on a piece of paper and seal it in an envelope? If we need to know, we can open the envelope," Peter said.

"Of course. It will be like your own personal 'break glass in case of emergency,'" Dr. Kasahara said, bringing a little lighthearted mood to the room.

With our decisions made, there was nothing left to do but try to stay calm and keep the baby inside as long as possible.

Chapter 6

2008

Hearing I was pregnant was thrilling. Getting to see the baby on ultrasound was icing on the cake. Even though the test results were conclusive, my doctor wanted to do an ultrasound just to make sure everything was looking good.

As soon as the wand was inserted, my doctor broke into a smile—something I had never seen him do before. He talked me through what he was seeing, "a nice gestational sac with a strong heartbeat on the right." Then he turned the probe to the left side of my uterus and showed me the other nice gestational sac with a strong heartbeat.

The IUI was a success—a little too much of a success. Even though letrozole was supposed to stimulate just one egg to drop, my body had other plans and dropped two eggs. I was pregnant with twins.

I asked my doctor a few times if he was sure—hoping, perhaps, that he had just made a mistake and the one baby was moving around so quickly he mistook one sac for two. The idea of twins terrified me. Not only would Peter and I be outnumbered by our children, but I also wasn't sure if my body could even handle a twin pregnancy. Two babies meant twice the risk.

Once I got over the shock, I rushed into the hallway to give Peter a call.

"Honey, can you talk?"

"Yeah, what's up?" Peter said, obviously a little distracted.

"Well, I got the results of the official pregnancy test . . ."

"Let me guess, you're pregnant?" he said, a little proud of himself.

"Yep. I'm pregnant. *Really* pregnant," I replied.

"OK."

"As in *really, really* pregnant."

Pause.

"You there?" I asked with a giant smirk on my face.

"What are you trying to tell me?" he asked, totally confused by what was happening.

"Well, apparently when you are pregnant with twins, your hCG levels really rise quickly."

Silence.

"Honey. You there?" I asked.

"Twins? Twins. We are having twins?" Peter had finally composed himself enough to answer me.

The rest of our phone call was spent listening to Peter's stream of unanswerable questions: "How the hell did this happen?" "Can you carry twins to term?" "How are we going to tell Irene?" "Can we handle twins?" I finally convinced him that we would talk about it further once he came home.

My next task was to tell my parents. I think I had even more fun telling them than I did telling Peter. I took in a deep breath and entered their house looking as somber as I could.

"Hi," I said with as much of a depressing tone as I could muster.

"Oh, honey. It was a false positive?" my mom asked. She was trying not to tear up.

Just as my dad was opening his mouth to say something, I burst into a huge smile. I could see the relief wash across their faces as they realized I was pregnant.

"Melissa! That was not nice," my mom yelled.

"I'm sorry. I couldn't help it," I replied. "As a peace offering, would you like to see the ultrasound picture?"

"You have a picture?" Mom asked as she was already moving over to make space for me on the couch between her and Dad.

"OK, see this here. That is your grandkid . . ." I said, pointing to the sac on the left. After a good long pause, I went in for the kill: ". . . and that over there is your other grandkid."

I was greeted by blank stares. Both my parents were processing what I had told them. Finally, my dad broke the silence and said with a straight face, "I can't afford to help send three grandkids to college!"

Chapter 7

2010

With the decision to keep the pregnancy going, it was time to do some mental preparation for the fact that we were going to have a premature baby. Neither of us knew anything about having a preemie. Luckily, I remembered a former coworker of mine, Kawika, had a two-year-old girl who was born at just twenty-nine weeks. We figured talking to someone who had been through what we were facing would be helpful. I also thought Peter would benefit from talking to another dad who understood exactly what decisions he was being asked to make.

Thank God I remembered their story. Kawika comforted Peter and gave him hope that he was making the right decisions. Kawika's wife, Jenny, whom I had forgotten was a registered nurse, spent time on the phone with me, asking lots of questions about what the doctors were giving me. The main thing she wanted to know was if they had given me the steroid shots for women at risk of delivering a premature baby.

"Steroids? What steroids?" I asked.

"The steroids help the baby's lungs develop faster in preparation for birth. You want to have at least two doses before you give birth if you can," Jenny replied with such authority and urgency.

"Nobody has talked to me about steroids at all," I told her. I felt so uninformed and mad. Why hadn't anyone talked to me about this?

"I am not hanging up until you get someone on this." Jenny's insistence was comforting. Having a nurse, who was also a preemie mom, in my corner was giving me hope.

I pushed the call button, and within moments my nurse, Tamara, appeared.

"Tamara, I want the steroids," I said, trying to sound like I knew what I was talking about.

Jenny chimed in with all the authority of a registered nurse, telling Tamara exactly what steroids I was talking about. Jenny was not pushy, but she was clear that we needed a discussion with someone about the steroids right away.

I was looking at Tamara and could see she was not going to argue with us, and possibly that she was even in agreement. Tamara had been my nurse when I first got put into Trendelenburg. She was warm and kind, and I felt safe with her in my room.

"I will page the perinatologist. He is the one who can order the steroids." *Great,* I thought, *Dr. Doom to the rescue.*

Satisfied that things were in motion, Jenny said goodbye but promised she was around anytime to answer questions and help advocate for us from afar.

Dr. Doom took his time answering Tamara's page. It may have only been thirty minutes, but it felt like hours. As soon as he walked into the room, the tension rose and I could feel my heart racing.

"I understand you want to start a course of betamethasone," Dr. Doom said in his condescending tone. "I don't know who you have been talking to, but studies have not shown much positive impact until a baby reaches at least twenty-four weeks, and there are potential adverse side effects that could further threaten the baby if the shots are given too early."

"Since you already think this is a doomed pregnancy, what is the harm in trying?" Peter responded, doing his best to hold in his rage.

"Well, if you insist on trying to keep this pregnancy going, and are willing to risk harming the . . ."

"We insist," Peter cut him off. My face was contorted with rage, and Peter could see I was about to unleash my anger.

Dr. Doom muttered something and walked out.

A moment later Tamara poked her head inside my room. "He signed the form. The steroids will be here soon."

Not ten minutes later Tamara came back in with a new drug to hang on my IV stand. Once the bag was empty, there was nothing else to do except worry, wait, and watch the monitors tracking my contractions.

Chapter 8

2008

Being pregnant with twins was hard. I was already considered a high-risk pregnancy, and when you added twins to the mix, the risk was even higher. I was on limited bed rest from the moment we found out I was pregnant. The "limited" became mandatory if I started to bleed—which I did often. With the bleeding also came daily progesterone shots.

"Christ, that is a big needle!" Peter exclaimed, like this was the first time he'd had to give me a shot.

"Thanks, that helped calm me down," I snorted sarcastically, annoyed that he had reminded me once again how big the damn needle was. "Do you think this time you could go a little faster? The hesitation just builds up the suspense and makes me all tense."

"I'm doing my best here, Melissa. This isn't fun for me."

"Fun for you? Fun for . . . Jesus, Peter. I am the one having the big needle shoved into my ass cheek!"

What little intimacy Peter and I shared was not improved by these injections. It's not like we were having lots of sex anyway—between bed rest and the growing tension between us, the last thing I was interested in was sex. Of course, I am not sure sticking a needle in my ass was something that increased Peter's desire for sex either.

I went to my nine-week ultrasound alone. Peter had to work, and I was tired of having to ensure the spotlight was on him. I wanted to make sure the twins and I were the focus of this appointment, not Peter and how he was feeling about everything.

Dr. Chetkowski was surprised to see me alone.

"Isn't Peter coming?" he asked. I just silently shook my head.

"OK then, let's get you on the table and take a look at these twins of yours."

As I slipped my legs into the stirrups, I chuckled at the lobster-shaped oven mitts covering the cold metal.

"OK, deep breath and you will feel pressure as I insert the wand."

I inhaled, closed my eyes, and waited to hear the heartbeats of the twins.

"Hmm," Dr. Chetkowski uttered. I felt the wand move. Left, then right, then left again.

I opened my eyes and turned my head to look at the doctor. His brow was furrowed. He was looking intently at the monitor. Just as I was about to speak, he turned to me.

"I am sorry," Dr. Chetkowski said. "I never had a good feeling about that fetus."

"I don't understand."

"The twin on the left has stopped developing."

"I . . . I don't understand," I said again as tears began to stream down my face.

"Melissa, I told you I didn't like the idea of you carrying more than one child. Your uterus is just not built for more than one."

"But there were two. What happened?" I asked.

"The second fetus never had the strongest of heartbeats. It was always smaller than the other fetus. I just don't think it was as strong as the other."

I began crying more now as the reality hit me that my twin pregnancy was over and I only had one baby left.

"I know this is hard for you to understand, but I think this is a good thing. You now have a much better chance of carrying the other baby to term."

It's true that I hadn't wanted twins, but the past few weeks had allowed me to get used to the idea. Now I had lost one of my babies and was going to have to adjust to the idea that I was only going to have one baby.

"So, now what?" I asked. "What do we do now?"

"You have two choices. We can do a selective D&C, or we can wait and let your body reabsorb the fetus."

It seemed rather macabre to know there was a dead baby in my uterus next to a living one. I was worried that this would complicate my pregnancy even more, possibly putting the healthy baby at risk. Dr. Chetkowski did his best to reassure me.

"Leaving the dead fetus in there will not put the healthy baby at risk," Dr. Chetkowski explained. "In my opinion, the safest course of action is to do nothing and let your body do what is necessary."

I turned my head away from the doctor and was now staring at the wall. My throat was dry, and my eyes stung from the tears. I pulled my hands to my face, and after a brief moment, I rolled back over, my hands still over my face.

"I'll take the safest option. I can't lose both of them."

Chapter 9

2010

Near the end of our first full day in Labor & Delivery, the nurses told us to bring stuff from home that would make me more comfortable: laptop, pregnancy pillow, toothbrush, cell phone charger, hand lotion, lip balm, and, of course, a picture of Irene. Room 8 in Labor & Delivery was going to be my home until I was stable enough to move to antepartum or until I gave birth. Either way, I was not leaving Alta Bates hospital until I had delivered a baby.

While Peter was gone picking up my home items, I took the time to set some goals. The first goal was easy. I had to make it to that critical twenty-four-week mark—just three days away. That goal felt attainable, even easy. I decided I also needed to set a more challenging goal. Kawika and Jenny's baby was born at twenty-nine weeks. I wanted to beat them, so I made my long-term goal thirty weeks. That was a nice round number and would mean six weeks in the hospital before delivering.

When Peter came back, I told him my goals.

"I know we will get to the twenty-four-week mark, but I have decided I am not going to have this baby until I am thirty weeks pregnant."

"Um, Melissa, you know you don't know that," Peter responded.

"Like hell I don't. I. Will. Not. Have. This. Baby. YET!" I angry-cried at Peter.

He decided the safest thing was to let me believe that I had total control over things. At the same time, he worked hard to keep me focused on the short-term goal.

The button the nurses had given me to mark any contractions now felt like a security blanket. I clutched it in my hands and would not let go. The button helped make me feel like I was in control. I was the one pressing it, letting everyone know if I was contracting or not. I felt powerful holding that button. I channeled my hopes for making it to thirty weeks into that button. My desire for things to be OK was manifesting in my grip. I was willing myself not to need to push it. Luckily, by the end of the second day, the magnesium sulfate and Procardia began to work, and my contractions had slowed to just one per hour, if that.

With my contractions more under control, Peter left the hospital to have a difficult talk with Irene. He let her know that Mommy and Baby were sick and that we would be staying in the hospital for a while. He did his best to reassure her that we would be OK, but Irene was scared. What four-year-old in just her second week of kindergarten wouldn't be?

It was hard for Peter to be positive, being as scared as he was. Irene asked if they could sleep at my parents' house. She wanted to be surrounded by as many people that loved her as possible.

While Irene and Peter had their sleepover at my parents', I spent my third night in the hospital alone.

It wasn't as bad as I thought it would be. My contractions had all but stopped, but I was still upside down and hooked up to the magnesium sulfate. This meant the headache I had gotten my first few hours in the hospital would not go away, and I was now taking a lot of painkillers. In all honesty, I was happy to be drugged.

Since arriving at the hospital, I had been hit with so much over-whelming news that being blissed out on painkillers was a nice break from all the worry and fear.

One day shy of the twenty-four-week goal brought a whole new set of issues. My lower back realized the crazy position I was in was not ending anytime soon, and there was nothing I could do to get comfortable. I wiggled and kept changing positions—first lying on my back, then on my left side facing whoever was visiting, then on my right staring at the sink. I shoved pillow after pillow under my side, between my legs, under my knees, and in whatever combination might help. The doctors changed the painkiller to something stronger in hopes of settling me down. They were concerned that all my moving and wiggling could cause my water to break, taking my situation from critical to . . . What is there after critical?

If my back was not enough of a problem, my headaches worsened. The combination of the magnesium sulfate and the blood rushing to my head was a perfect one-two punch. I hit miserable that day, but that did nothing to sway me from sticking to my long-term goal of staying in that bed for six weeks. My mom always joked that the stubborn gene passed on from her grandmother to her mother to her and then to me only strengthened with each successive generation. I was counting on my mom's theory to be right.

Outside of sheer stubbornness I knew there was one thing I would need to keep myself on track for reaching my goal: better access to the outside world. Typing on a laptop while tilted at a thirty-degree angle was nearly impossible. Peter jumped at the opportunity to run to the nearest Apple store and get me an iPad. That device became my lifeline, allowing me to stay entertained with streaming movies and TV shows and connected with my friends and family through the Internet. I didn't have the energy to talk on the phone, so Facebook and email were the only ways that I could connect with my friends on the outside.

With my condition as critical as it was, and the order from my doctor to stay calm, I was not letting many people visit. It wasn't just because I needed the room quiet so I could visualize peaceful waterfalls to maintain a peaceful demeanor. I was also embarrassed because the magnesium sulfate caused massive hot flashes, which led to soaking sweats, which led to overwhelming body odor and terrible hair. I had some pride, and it was telling me to keep people away.

The only people I did let visit were Peter, Irene, my parents, and my oldest and dearest friend, Stephanie. Just as she did with Irene, Stephanie was going to act as my birth coach with this baby. Her visits helped brighten my day, just a little.

The one person who I wanted to see beyond everyone else was Irene. I hadn't seen her since dropping her off at school four days prior. Peter was supposed to bring her to see me after school had ended. As the day wore on, I got impatient waiting for Irene's arrival. I asked my mom, who was keeping me company, what time it was every few minutes.

I heard them coming before I saw them. Irene was talking to her dad about something that had happened in her kindergarten classroom.

As soon as they got to the door to my room, Irene saw me and screamed, "Mama!"

Despite her elation at seeing me, it was obvious from the look on her face and the way she hesitated at the door to my room she was scared by how I looked. Peter had done his best to prepare her, but honestly, how do you prepare a four-year-old for seeing her mommy lying at a thirty-degree angle with monitors hooked up to her?

"It's OK, nugget. Come here!" I did my best to make my voice feel strong and reassuring. "I need an Irene hug."

She looked at her dad and then to my mom for reassurance. They both smiled at her, and she began to walk toward me slowly. As soon as she was within reaching distance, I put my hand out and pulled her closer. The tension in her body left, and her face relaxed. She came right up to the edge of the bed and asked, "Can I get in bed with you?"

"God yes!" I smiled, and she climbed up and rested her head on my pillow.

"I'm falling!" she said through her giggles as she tried to settle.

I wrapped my arms around her. "I've got you, baby. I will not let you fall," I whispered as I nuzzled into the nape of her neck.

"Tell me something funny that happened at kindergarten today," I asked.

"I got to bring home the class racoon!" Irene exclaimed.

"I'm sorry, there is a racoon in my house?"

"Not a real one, silly. A stuffed racoon. I can bring him to meet you tomorrow."

"I would love that!"

We stayed like that for a while. Irene never asked how I was or when I would come home; I think that was too much for her. She stayed long enough to charm the nurses into bringing her two containers of Jello, and then Peter took her home—to spend the night in her own house and her own bed.

It was hard watching Irene leave.

"I see you tomorrow!" Irene squeaked with the adorable Mickey Mouse voice kids her age have.

Blowing me kisses from the door, Irene called out, "I love you, Mama," and then waltzed out of the room. I rode the high of her visit for the rest of that night.

Chapter 10

2008

We were all gathered in the conference room for a brainstorming session on our latest corporate video project. There must have been ten of us crammed into that room. My job as the director of production was to keep the conversation moving and the budget top of mind. This was my first day back since losing one of the twins. I hadn't told anyone except my boss and my friend Jennifer what had happened. I just did not want to deal with the pity glances.

As the conversation turned to CGI gorillas, I felt a sudden urge to pee. I excused myself, and as I walked down the hallway to the bathroom, I felt what I can only describe as a big water balloon full of blood rupture in my pelvis. Blood ran down to my knees, and I felt giant clots pass as well. I half waddled and half ran the rest of the way, leaving a trail of blood behind me on the office carpeting. Once in the bathroom, I locked myself in the nearest stall.

I pulled my pants down, took a deep breath, and looked down to see what had passed. I was convinced I was going to see a fetus in my underwear. I just didn't see how with all of that blood and all the large clots I felt passing out of me, I didn't lose the baby. I couldn't really make anything out because there was so much blood, so I sat on the toilet—weeping and paralyzed with fear about what to do next.

After a few minutes, a coworker entered the bathroom to fix her hair. I could see her through a crack in the stall door and watched her expression change as she noticed the trail of blood on the floor. I tried my best to suppress my sobs, but that just made it worse. I finally managed to get enough air in my lungs to whisper, "Can you please find Jennifer and have her come here?" Jennifer knew about my losing one twin, and I was sure she could handle the situation.

Relieved that I had asked for someone other than her to help me, this poor girl tore out of that bathroom, and within moments, Jennifer appeared and took control. I heard her locking the entrance door to the bathroom.

"Honey, are you OK?" she asked.

I just cried in response.

I could hear her pulling paper towels out and could see her wiping the floor.

"Melissa, I need you to tell me something. Did you hurt yourself, or is this related to your pregnancy?"

"I think I lost the other baby," I sobbed.

"Give me Peter's number," she said gently but firmly.

I somehow managed to give her the number.

I could only hear snippets of her call with Peter. I heard "come now," "lots of blood," and "I'm calling 911 next." When she hung up, Jennifer moved closer to the door and said, "Peter is on his way. I am calling an ambulance. You lost a lot of blood."

Just then there was a knock on the bathroom door. The news of a bleeding person in the bathroom had spread quickly. The CEO of the company wanted to know what was going on.

"You can't come in. Just call an ambulance. Tell them it sounds like a miscarriage," Jennifer said through the locked door.

"I have no pants!" I called out.

"What?" she asked.

"I have no pants to wear out of here. They are soaked in blood."

I heard Jennfier on the phone again, this time to the reception-ist. "Go to the pharmacy across the street and buy sweatpants and underwear for Melissa." As soon as she hung up, Jennifer came back to the stall door.

"How we doing in there? Are you remembering to breathe?"

I sobbed.

"Do you want me to call anyone else?" she asked.

"My dad. Call my dad. He works around the corner." I man-aged to give her my dad's number. That call was even shorter than the one with Peter. All I heard was "I will text you."

I felt another huge gush of blood and clots. "Oh God!" I yelped.

"Breathe. Just breathe."

I never opened the door for Jennifer, but it felt like she was next to me, hugging me and holding me up the entire time.

Suddenly, there was a banging on the door, and I could hear Peter calling my name. Jennifer unlocked the door and let him in.

I could hear him gasp.

"I know . . . it's a lot of blood," Jennifer answered.

"Melissa . . ."

At the sound of his voice, I cried harder.

"Melissa, can you open the door?" Peter asked.

Another gush of blood. I wailed. "I am scared to look in the toilet," I told him.

"You don't need to. Let the paramedics do that when they get here," Peter replied.

The three of us stayed in that bathroom, Peter leaning against the locked stall door, Jennifer cleaning up the blood on the floor, and me on the toilet, covered in blood and alternating between crying hysterically and quietly staring at the back of the stall door.

There was a big ding on the door. I would fixate on it, trying to figure out how the ding was created. Had someone punched the door in anger, thrown their phone, tripped and fallen? It was a nice distraction. It was calming to stare into the ding.

There was a loud banging on the door. This time it was the three firefighters and two paramedics. Jennifer told them all that she knew, which wasn't much. One of the paramedics knocked on the stall door and told me it was time to open the door. I was mortified by the trouble I was causing. I apologized to the paramedics for having to deal with the mess.

"It's OK. Can you stand?" the male paramedic asked me.

"I'm scared. What if my baby is in the toilet?" I cried. I didn't want my last memory of this pregnancy to be a dead baby lying in a bloody toilet.

Chapter II

2010

Even though I didn't want visitors, it didn't mean I wanted to be alone. With my new iPad, I was able to immerse myself in the love and support of friends and family. As news of my situation spread, the amount of emails and encouraging posts grew.

One of the biggest challenges I faced while in Trendelenburg was trying to figure out how to eat. Lying down and eating is hard. Lying down and eating with your head below your feet is really, really hard. I ended up licking more food off my pillow than I got into my mouth. It didn't help that I kept ordering things like soup and oatmeal.

So, here I was, trapped in bed, licking food off my pillow, suffering from terrible headaches and back pain, drenched in sweat. I tried to focus on the positives of having magnesium sulfate being poured into my body. Aside from stopping preterm contractions, studies have shown that it can help speed up lung development and protect the brain from damage in premature babies. Unfortunately, the nasty side effects it had on adults were starting to add up. I needed a new gown every twenty minutes because I was sweating so badly. Since I was on restricted movement, I had to rely on my nurses to get me a new gown. It was a humbling experience having to rely on others to do something as simple as changing my clothing. It was also not an option to change the sheets on the bed or allow me to get up and shower. I think by the time Tuesday rolled around I smelled about as good as I felt.

Then again, it was Tuesday. My short-term goal. The day when my baby went from being nonviable to viable. This was the day I had been focused on. This was the day Dr. Doom was sure I would never reach. This was the day that meant my baby might actually live, the greatest Tuesday in my entire life.

Now that we had reached twenty-four weeks and crossed over to the world of viability, Peter and I were able to breathe a little easier. We knew the statistics were now more encouraging, and if we had to have the baby today, at least there was a chance he or she would not just survive, but survive with a good quality of life.

I became more determined to reach my long-term goal. I decided I could tolerate anything if it meant holding this baby in longer. I had been transferred to a special bed for people who are going to be bedridden for a long time; it was more padded and made of a material that breathed better. I sank into the comfort of the new bed and relaxed—for about twenty minutes. The reality was nothing could make me comfortable. I was still in Trendelenburg and was still getting an IV drip of magnesium sulfate.

My current day nurse, Beth, was starting her second day with me, and I was relieved to see her. We had gotten along the previous day, and I felt very comfortable with her. How could I not like her? The first thing she did was to find a way to give me a sponge bath to celebrate hitting the twenty-four-week mark. I am not sure what I enjoyed more: washing my armpits or getting my hair washed.

Irene appreciated it too.

"Mama!" Irene exclaimed excitedly. "I can't smell you anymore."

Leave it to a four-year-old to say what everyone else was thinking.

But when Beth arrived for her shift on Wednesday, my contractions had started up again. They were not as strong as they had been before the magnesium sulfate, but I found myself pushing the button more than once an hour. Beth began to spend more and more time in the room with me. She wanted to see how I looked as opposed to what the monitors said. She became so concerned, she asked the charge nurse to reassign her other two patients to another nurse, as she felt I needed constant monitoring. At around 11 a.m., Beth decided to "check me," a delicate way of saying she needed to look under my gown to see if everything was OK. To my horror, Beth saw what looked like amniotic fluid on the sheet.

She called Dr. Kasahara, who ordered a bedside ultrasound. The results were mixed. My sac was still intact (yeah!) and had moved back into the uterus (yeah!). Unfortunately, my sac was now stretched tightly across my cervix and was oozing amniotic fluid.

"Imagine a soaking wet dish towel stretched as tight as possible across the opening of a glass," Dr. Kasahara explained. "Your sac is the dish towel, and your cervix is the glass."

"So, this is bad, right?" I asked, starting to understand.

"Yes. Aside from the fact that you are losing amniotic fluid, your sac is in danger of rupturing at any moment."

Before I could ask anything, Dr. Kasahara added, "And from what I can see, the umbilical cord is located right at the bottom of the sac, close to the cervix. This means if the sac ruptures, the cord would be sucked out and compressed, putting your baby as risk."

"Oh my God. Then what?"

"We would be in an emergency situation. We would need to do a crash C-section, and we would not have a lot of time to do it."

I started picturing scenes from *ER* and *Grey's Anatomy*: a patient on a gurney being rushed down a hallway with a resident sitting on top of the mom in labor, sticking her hand up the woman's vagina, trying to keep the cord from being compressed and cutting off oxygen to the baby.

Peter and I now had to have the "gut-wrenching decision" discussion with the doctors again. This time, Dr. Doom's partner was on duty, and he provided a much more optimistic outlook.

"So, we are now at the twenty-four-week mark. This changes a lot of things," the doctor proclaimed.

I smiled. I knew what this meant. We were now in the land of viability.

"So, now what?" Peter asked.

"Well, for starters . . . congratulations. This baby has a much better chance at survival—even if you gave birth today."

"Thank you—your partner told us to give up," Peter said half angrily and half defiantly.

"I'm sorry you had the experience. I am. But now there is no question this is a viable fetus, so let's talk about next steps."

I loved hearing that. *Next steps.* "Yes, please!" I called out.

Despite all the good news, the decisions we had to make were still scary. Since we were still between twenty-four and twenty-five weeks, it was up to us if we wanted extraordinary measures to be taken if needed.

"Yes! My God, yes. I haven't laid here like this to let the baby just die after birth." I was shocked I even had to say this.

"OK. I figured, but I did have to ask," the doctor replied. "We also need to know, if we need to do a C-section, do you consent to the surgery?"

"Like I have a choice?" I half asked and half giggled. It seemed odd to me that they would need to do a C-section for such a tiny baby. I honestly didn't care how they got the baby out. I just wanted him or her to live.

With our signatures on a few pieces of paper, the perinatologist and ultrasound technician left the room. We were back to waiting.

The joy of hearing "survive" was short-lived. The rest of the day was awful. My head was throbbing, and my back and hips felt like they were on fire. I was no longer able to adjust my position or even move without first calling a nurse into the room. To make matters worse, I was starving! Licking hospital food off my pillow for five days had left me a little undernourished, and now I was not allowed to eat or drink anything since we had consented to the C-section. My only source of fluids was an IV. Just like any other surgery, the anesthesiologists require an empty stomach just in case they have to put you fully under. Since I was at risk for a crash C-section, this meant the chances of me having general anesthesia were high. In hindsight, I should have known that the end of my pregnancy was near. While I was getting fluids to stay hydrated, I was not getting any sort of nutritional support.

Peter and Irene arrived for her after-school visit. Nothing lit up my room quite like Irene's arrival. She bounded into my room, skipping and clutching a stuffed racoon.

"Mommy! I brought you the class racoon," she squealed.

I couldn't help but laugh. Her joy at this stuffed racoon was infectious.

"I get to keep her for a whole week! And I can take pictures with her and tell all my friends what we did together."

Irene was talking so fast I was unable to follow after that. Instead, I allowed myself to be lost in her joy and giant toothy smile. For just a brief moment I was transported away from my hospital bed, stress, and pain into the world of a happy, carefree four-year-old.

As soon as Irene left, my joy was replaced with sadness. I was missing so much being in the hospital. Irene had made a bunch of new friends, and I had only met one of them. I felt disconnected from all of her new experiences. I was also disappointed because I had planned on volunteering in Irene's classroom once a week until the baby was born. Now I knew I would be lucky to make it to her classroom at all. I wanted to get out of that hospital and go to the school to see Irene in her element. I knew the experiences I was missing I would never get back.

Chapter 12

2008

I was frozen in place. I knew I needed to stand up, but I just couldn't. My legs were trembling—partly from sitting on the toilet that long and partly from the massive blood loss. One of the paramedics put his arm around me and told me I had get up. He needed to examine me, and they had to see what was in the toilet. Slowly, with his help, I moved from sitting on the toilet to sitting on the floor, making sure not to look into the toilet bowl. He collected what he could from the toilet and sealed it in a bag. He and his partner lifted me up on a wheelchair, wrapped me in a blanket, and wheeled me out of the bathroom.

It took about an hour from the time we were wheeled into the hospital for an ultrasound technician to arrive. Privately, I began my own mourning process, saying goodbye to the last twin.

The ultrasound technician was all business once he arrived. He settled into his chair, slathered my belly with gel, and got to work. I was too scared to look at the monitor. The tech was quiet for a second before exclaiming: "I have never seen a dead baby move like that!"

"What?" I eeked out as Peter's grip on my hand tightened.

"Here, look," the tech said, pointing to the monitor.

"Oh my God," Peter cried. "Melissa, I can see the baby moving around."

My tears of anguish stopped, and tears of joy began to flow. The hot burn of bile that was rising in my throat receded and was replaced with the warmth of hope. I was still pregnant. I have no idea how, but as clear as day you could see the baby moving around on the ultrasound monitor.

"I want to go home," I said to Peter. "I'm just so tired."

I was exhausted from the emotional outpouring of the past couple of hours. Plus, I had lost a significant amount of blood. I would celebrate still being pregnant after I was home and took a nap.

Even though Dr. Chetkowski had predicted that the dead fetus either would be reabsorbed into my body or would come out when I delivered the healthy baby, my body had decided on a different path and expelled it. There was no sign of the dead fetus on the ultrasound, and the staff at the hospital felt it was the most logical explanation for what had happened.

My discharge instructions from the hospital were simple: go home and get comfy. I was now on bed rest for the rest of my pregnancy, possibly six months. I was too tired to process what this would mean for Irene, my job, my marriage, and my sanity. I was just relieved to be going home with a baby still inside of me.

That was on a Wednesday.

My first appointment with my OB was not until the following Tuesday of a holiday weekend. Despite the excitement of the day, when I called to see if I could get in sooner, Dr. Kasahara didn't have any openings.

"Doesn't she keep a few appointments for emergencies?" I asked.

"Since you have not been here before, she can't bump you up."

"But I was in the hospital yesterday. Doesn't that give me some sort of priority?" I was now pleading with the staff.

"She has seen the ultrasound and is not worried. If your status changes, call back."

In my exhausted state this sounded like bullshit to me, but I was too tired to fight anymore.

I crawled into bed and fell sound asleep.

My first day of bed rest was boring but easy. The bleeding had stopped, and I was feeling stronger. My brother, Brian, who was a reporter living in Costa Rica at the time, was arriving that night for an extended visit. It had been almost a year since I had seen him, and I was really looking forward to some sibling time.

As excited as I was to see Brian, Irene was even more excited. Even though he only popped up every now and then, her tío, as he liked to be called, found a way to be close: no matter where in the world Brian went, he sent Irene a postcard. Although he didn't have kids of his own, Brian filled the role of "fun uncle" like a pro.

I knew having Brian here would be a wonderful distraction for Irene. I could see in Irene's face that she was worried about me, and also confused by my new, stricter activity restrictions. Breakfast in bed was cute, but Irene wanted me to come upstairs and play. Even at a mature four, Irene had a hard time understanding why Mom was not getting out of bed. I was hoping that my brother's presence would give her something positive to focus on.

"Remember, Tío will be here when you get home from school, and he has so much fun stuff planned for you," I told Irene as she picked out an outfit to wear to school.

"Like what, Mama?" Irene asked with a smile.

"Well, I know he wants to take you to Fentons for an ice cream date."

"Yeah! Ice cream. Will you come with us?" Irene asked hopefully.

I wanted so much to say yes. "I'm sorry, kiddo. I wasn't invited," I told her. "Tío wants you and the ice cream all to himself."

This seemed to work. Irene liked the idea of solo time with Tío.

Within twenty minutes of Peter and Irene leaving, I started to feel contractions. As the day wore on, the contractions worsened. By late afternoon, I was in too much pain to stand. I called my OB's office and finally got to talk to the doctor.

"I know we have not met, but something is wrong," I told her.

"Based on the labs I have seen, there is nothing to worry about," she replied.

"But I am contracting again. A lot!" I cried.

"Well, you are only fourteen weeks along, so there isn't much we can do," Dr. Kasahara said emotionlessly. "If you are that concerned, your only recourse is to go to the emergency room."

Chapter 13

2010

The next day it was clear my plan of making it to thirty weeks was slipping away. My contractions became stronger and more consistent, making it even harder for me to get comfortable. My best friend, Stephanie, and her husband, Mike, had come by for a visit. Every time I had a contraction, my face showed it before I even pressed the button. Steph and Mike didn't say anything, but I could see with each contraction they would look at each other with worry.

Steph had only planned on staying for an hour, but that hour turned to two and then was heading toward three.

"You don't have to stay," I said, trying to sound strong.

"Like hell I don't," Steph replied. "I am not leaving you here alone."

"If she stays, I stay," Mike added.

"I am pretty shitty company."

"I love you too," Steph responded.

We weren't really talking much at this point, as the contractions were getting more frequent and more intense. I had my eyes closed, trying to will my body to behave. But with each contraction, my gasps of pain became louder, and involuntary tears were streaming down my face. I knew my pregnancy was coming to an end, and soon.

My nurse, Beth, joined Steph and Mike at their bedside vigil. My parents were on their way, with Peter and Irene close behind. Before the crowd arrived, Beth checked me again, and found a considerable amount of amniotic fluid on the bed. This, plus the increase in my contractions, was enough for her. She paged the OB on call, Dr. Wharton. As luck would have it, this was the ONE day during my entire hospitalization that Dr. Kasahara was off and out of town at a family event. We had never met Dr. Wharton, and he knew nothing about us or my history.

Before the doctor would even see me, he ordered a new bedside ultrasound. He told Beth he wanted a full and current picture of what was going on before he would come up.

While we were waiting for the ultrasound machine, my mom and dad arrived. Walking into the room, my parents took one look at Stephanie's face and knew there was a problem. My mom could read Stephanie like a book, something that comes from having been a part of her life since birth. No words were spoken. Just when my dad was about to ask what was going on, the ultrasound tech arrived and kicked everyone out. I was left alone with my nurse, the ultrasound tech, and a belly covered in warm gel. I wished that Peter or my parents could be with me. I knew the news I was going to get was not good.

As soon as the ultrasound tech left, Stephanie, Mike, and my parents came back into the room. Dr. Wharton followed them soon after.

Dr. Wharton had a warm face and he carried himself with the right amount of professionalism and compassion. After briefly taking the time to meet everyone in the room and get a sense of their role in my life, he came over to my bedside, knelt down so we were eye to eye, and said, "It's time. I know you don't want to hear this, but the ultrasound is very concerning."

My eyes closed and I was unable to speak. I just nodded.

"The gestational sac is no longer fully in your uterus."

I knew what that meant. But Dr. Wharton wasn't done.

"In addition, part of the umbilical cord is included in the portion of the sac that is outside your uterus."

Everyone in the room was quiet. I could hear my mom breathing deeper. My dad shuffled his feet.

"Melissa, there is more. The baby is in a breech position. These three things together have taken your situation to critical."

Just then I heard Irene's voice in the hallway. Peter pushed the door open, and as he entered the room, he looked from person to person. Seeing the crowd and the concerned expressions on everyone's faces, he knew something was wrong. His body stiffened, and his grip on Irene's hand loosened.

"Irene . . . I have great news! You and I are going on an adventure," my dad said without any prompting.

"Ooooo." Irene clapped.

"I need a hamburger."

"Milkshake!" Irene squealed.

"And curly fries," my dad added.

"Wait, give Mommy a kiss hello before you leave," I said, trying not to cry. She wrapped her little arms around my neck and I buried my nose in her hair.

I mouthed "Thank you" to my dad, and the two were off. Dad grabbed Stephanie on the way out and made her promise to keep him updated on everything that was going on. He knew relying on her was a safer bet than relying on my mom or Peter, who were clearly too distracted.

As soon as they were gone, Peter introduced himself to Dr. Wharton and asked what the hell was going on.

"Melissa's status has changed."

"What does that mean?" Peter asked as calmly as he could.

"Lying in Trendelenburg is no longer working. The sac is back outside the uterus," Dr. Wharton started to explain.

I shook my head and started to tear up. "How did this happen?" I asked. "I have not moved from this damn bed!"

Without answering me, Dr. Wharton continued to repeat everything he had just told me. Except this time, Dr. Wharton went further and said, "If the sac were to rupture now, the cord would be compressed, which would endanger the baby."

My ears began to ring. I had been through days of hell to get to this point, and now my body had failed me again, putting my baby in danger.

"We are at the point where it is more dangerous to leave the baby in than it is to take the baby out. We do not want this to become an emergency C-section. That puts both mom and baby at a higher risk for serious complications. Take a moment and talk, but I strongly encourage you to consent to the C-section. Now." Dr. Warthon's emphasis on the word "now" was clear.

The room emptied. Dr. Wharton, my mom, Mike, and Stephanie all stepped out. Peter and I were alone. After six days in Trendelenburg, the pain, the medications, and the fear caught up with me again, and I felt totally overwhelmed and unequipped to make this decision.

I looked at Peter. "What do we do?"

Chapter 14

2008

Since my contractions were not too bad, and I was alone and unable to drive, I decided to see how the day went before making any real decisions. My day home alone seemed to take forever. I watched TV as a distraction. Peter checked on me every hour, but he didn't come home early. Finally, around dinnertime, he and Irene arrived. Not long after, my parents and brother showed up for a family meal. I hid my pain and discomfort from everyone—partly to spare them, and partly so I could pretend this wasn't happening.

By Irene's bedtime, I could no longer pretend. It was clear I needed to get to the hospital, and Irene needed to get to my parents' house. As I dialed their number, I did my best to put on a happy voice. My dad was having none of it.

"What's wrong?" he said before I could even speak.

"Dad . . ." I managed to squeak out before I was overcome with tears.

Peter took the phone from me.

"Alan, Melissa is worse. We need to go to the hospital."

Before Peter was done talking, my dad said, "I'm on my way. What do you want me to tell Irene?"

"I have no idea."

"Tell her Tío wanted a sleepover." I had gathered myself enough to come up with a cover story that would not scare her.

Once Irene was happily out the door off to her big sleepover with Tío, Peter and I got in the car to head to the ER.

It was the Friday night of a long weekend—the worst time to be in the ER. There I was, contracting and lightly bleeding while surrounded by drunk frat guys who had been in a bar brawl. It took forever to get me into triage. All they did was ask me a few questions, take my temp and blood pressure, and then told us to wait back in the waiting room. Peter and I just sat there next to each other, barely talking. I was fourteen weeks pregnant and already in labor.

After three hours of sitting in the waiting room, we were called back. Peter pushed my wheelchair into the ultrasound room and helped me get onto the table. The tech squirted out a glob of gel on my belly, smooshed the wand down, and turned the monitor toward us. I took a deep breath and steeled myself before looking. Right away I knew the baby was OK. I could see my baby moving around, just like a normal healthy baby should.

"Don't tell us the sex of the baby," I said with relief. For one, there was still a baby. For another, we didn't know if we were having a boy or a girl and wanted to leave it that way.

"OK. But would you like to see the baby's toes?" the tech asked.

"Oh, yes. Show us everything else," Peter replied.

"There is one perfect, ten-fingered hand . . . Oh . . . and there is the other. Hmmm . . . Aha. A beautiful foot with ten toes. And there is the other." It was clear the ultrasound technician was having as much fun as we were.

"Thank you. This has been an awful week. I thought I lost the baby a few days ago, and with the contractions, I was sure that you were going to tell us there was no heartbeat."

"Usually when people come to the ER this early in the pregnancy, that is what I find. I am enjoying the good news part of my job right now."

Even though I was still contracting, the baby appeared very content and safe inside my uterus.

"It's kind of quiet right now. You guys can stay in here as long as I don't have another patient come in. I am sure the bed is more comfortable than that wheelchair."

After an hour or so, a transport nurse came to take me to my room in the ER—lucky number 13.

One of the nurses suggested that before I get into bed I should use the bathroom. Just as I sat down on the toilet, I felt another sudden rush of blood and looked down to see my previously healthy fetus hanging, ashen and still, out of my vagina. I let out a guttural scream and began weeping. Peter came running into the bathroom, took one look at me, and ran right out to get help. He ripped the door to the room open and screamed, "I need a doctor in here! RIGHT FUCKING NOW." This got the attention of about four nurses and a nurse practitioner who happened to be walking by.

There was nothing anyone could do. My twin pregnancy was over.

The sight of that fourteen-week-old fetus hanging out of me over the toilet bowl haunts me to this day. I sometimes close my eyes at night and see its perfectly formed hand gently touching its cute little button nose.

Because of my unique anatomy and the advanced stage of the pregnancy, I had to have a D&C to clean out the placenta that had not passed with the baby. Then I was sent to a room for a twenty-four-hour stay in the hospital. Luckily, the doctor who performed my D&C left explicit instructions that I was not to be sent to the Labor & Delivery floor where I would be surrounded by new moms and their babies. I was very grateful for this doctor's compassion. My mental state was fragile enough; the last thing I needed was to see a happy family with their baby.

After my brief stay, I was discharged and headed home to explain to my daughter that she was not going to be having a little brother or sister anytime soon.

Chapter 15

2010

B eth knocked on the door and told us she needed to reposition the baby's heartbeat monitor.

"What do you think?" we asked Beth.

"I can't really tell you what to do."

"We know. We trust you. Please. We need someone to reassure us," Peter replied.

"I have never met a doctor that would rush someone to deliver a baby at twenty-four weeks unless it was really necessary," Beth answered.

I smiled at Beth. "Thank you. That is just what we needed to hear."

"Can you tell Dr. Wharton that we agree and will sign the C-section papers?" Peter said.

She gave my hand a squeeze and left to get the process going. It was a relief to have the decision made. I had done all I could. I held this baby in for six days, getting him or her to the point of viability. My job was over.

My mom, Stephanie, and Mike came back into the room. I felt so much safer knowing they were there. I needed my mommy. I needed my best friend. I needed the unconditional love and support only this group of people could give me.

Once we decided to deliver, things moved quickly. Beth came in to clear some of the unnecessary equipment from the room. Stephanie and Mike packed up our belongings: two huge pregnancy pillows, flowers, cards, groceries, toiletries, power cords, computer, iPad, and pictures. Peter and my mom were on either side of me, doing their best to assure me that everything would be OK. I was doing my best to stay calm, but my thoughts darted between terror and relief. Even though I knew it was too early for the baby to be born, relief continued to wash over me. I could feel the tears streaming down my cheeks and the gentle way Stephanie wiped each one off.

Not five minutes after we signed the C-section authorization, a large team of nurses and doctors came in, led by Tamara, my champion nurse from my first few days in Labor & Delivery.

"Hi, Melissa. I am here to get you ready for your C-section."

"Are you going to be with me?" I asked, tearing up a little.

"I am the lead operating room nurse tonight."

The tears started to flow more steadily.

"That is the best news I have had all day."

"I was with you when you got here, and I will be with you until we get to meet your baby," Tamara replied.

I was going to have someone I knew and trusted on the medical team with me in the operating room. Just before they wheeled me out, Nurse Beth grabbed my hand and gave me a quick kiss on the cheek.

"You are going to do great. I will come see you in recovery if I can."

The ride from my room to the OR was surreal.

I had been in a bubble for six days, and now, suddenly, I was out in the harsh light of the hospital corridor, bombarded with new sounds and smells, and surrounded by a medical team. We moved down the hallway at a quick enough pace that I could feel a slight breeze on my face. I was still in Trendelenburg, something Tamara said would continue until it was time to put the epidural in. The doctors didn't want to do anything that would change the procedure from a C-section to an emergency C-section.

It was freezing in the operating room, and my teeth began to chatter. My eyes darted about, looking at the huge lights hanging above my head. It seemed to take forever for Peter to put on his scrubs and join me. In reality, it was probably less than thirty minutes. Being in the OR without any of my support system in sight allowed all of my defenses to crumble, and I began to cry uncontrollably. Everything I had suppressed for the past six days just came flooding out in a stream of tears, and there was nothing that any of the OR staff could do to calm me down. Just as I was about to cross over to hysterical, Tamara appeared from the other side of the room.

"What's wrong?" she asked calmly.

It was such a relief to see her that the ridiculousness of her question didn't even phase me.

"I'm scared."

"That's all? Everyone is scared in the OR. But it's going to be OK," Tamara replied before going back to setting up the surgical tray.

Maybe it was her matter-of-factness or the warmth in her eyes, but for some reason that little exchange calmed me long enough to get my tears under control.

Just as I began to breathe evenly, the anesthesiologist came in and told me it was time to get my epidural going. My first thought was, *Huh. I wonder how he will do that with me lying down in Trendelenburg.* That's when it hit me.

After six days of lying down with the blood rushing to my head, I was going to sit up.

They told me to go slow.

The process of getting me into a sitting position was simple enough. First, the nurses raised the head of my bed so I was flat. Then I swung my legs over the side of the bed, and this rush of freedom overtook me. I could feel air behind my legs. Not quite the "wind in your face as you drive down the highway with the windows down" rush of air, but it was the most I was going to get in an OR. That perspective change alone helped to improve my mood and relieve some of my back pain. Next, with one nurse behind me and another in front of me, they raised me to a sitting position. And then the room went black.

Within moments of sitting up, I passed out right into the arms of the nurse in front of me. I guess six days of blood rushing to one's head takes time to undo. They lay me back down, which is when I opened my eyes.

"So, aren't you guys going to help me up?" I asked a little impatiently.

"We will," said Nurse One.

"I'm ready—let's go," I said, a bit stronger.

"Yeah, we are going to wait a few more minutes. You did just pass out," added Nurse Two.

"Oh. Sorry. I . . . Oh," I muttered, totally embarrassed.

After a few minutes, and a very slow rise to a sitting-up position, I was finally looking at the world from an upright position. Every thirty seconds, a nurse would ask me how I was doing. Each time, I answered, "I'm sitting up!" Once they were satisfied that I was not going to pass out again, the anesthesiologist got to work.

I was not looking forward to getting the epidural. I remembered how much the epidural hurt when I had Irene and how scared I was about having such a huge needle inserted into my spine. One wrong move, and your birth story goes from beautiful to tragic. This time around, I was just so happy to be sitting up and moving around that I don't even remember the needle going in. There is something to be said for euphoric amnesia.

As soon as the operating room was ready, my husband was allowed in. Despite all the commotion from the doctors and nurses getting the operating room ready, Peter and I took a moment to make the last few prebaby decisions.

"We need a name," I said. "If anything goes wrong, the baby has to have a name."

"OK. We already know the boy name, right?" Peter reminded me. "Samuel William."

"Sam" for my mother's brother who had died a few years prior, and for my father's father, my stubborn grandfather who, at the age of eighty-eight, showed no signs of slowing down. "William" honored my mother's father as well as Peter's father.

"What if it's a girl?" I asked. "Do we go with Lillian Hazel or Hazel Lillian?"

Lillian was a name we loved, and Hazel was to honor Peter's great aunt who had died the previous year (to the day, it turned out) at the ripe old age of 104.

"Well, even if it's a girl, she is going to need all the help she can get. Let's name her Hazel," Peter replied.

We were in agreement: Samuel William for a boy, Hazel Lillian for a girl.

Next came the question of what Peter was supposed to do with himself once the baby was born. For me, it was clear what he needed to do: stick with the baby. The decision wasn't as clear for Peter. He didn't want to leave me alone in the operating room, but he also didn't want to leave our new baby alone. I did my best to reassure him.

"I have my mom and Stephanie. They will take care of me. I need you to be with our baby."

"I don't want to leave you," he whispered.

"I don't want you to either, but someone has to be taking pictures of that baby and sending reports back to me. How else do you think they will keep me in my recovery bed?"

"Fine. But I am on record not wanting to leave you," Peter reluctantly agreed.

"OK, it's time," Dr. Wharton told us. Just then, the door to the OR opened, and another team of doctors and nurses came flooding into the OR. At first, I thought this extra team was for me until the lead doctor on the team, Dr. Sandhu, introduced himself as the neonatologist. All of those people were there for my baby. It seemed like such a huge medical team for such a small person.

And that is when it started to hit me: my job was almost done. I had done everything I could for my baby—holding on to him or her against all odds to make it to the critical twenty-four-week mark. Now my baby's fate was going to be in the hands of this medical team. All I knew about them was that their leader was Dr. Sandhu and he had the kindest eyes I had ever seen.

This C-section seemed longer than the one I had with Irene. Peter sat there with me, holding my hand and stroking my forehead as I wept. It was hard not to weep at this point. There had been so much heaped on us in the past few days . . . hell, the past few years. It was all coming down to this moment. I was having my baby. This was the last time I would ever be pregnant, and there was a possibility the baby would not survive being born. It was all just too much.

Then we heard it. A tiny little cry. It was more of a squeak than a cry, really. It was the most wonderful and beautiful sound in the world. I hadn't expected to hear my baby, given how early he or she was being born. But the baby did cry, and it was like the baby was reassuring me by saying, "I am here! I am going to be OK, Mom."

Dr. Wharton told Peter to stand up and take a look. With tears in his eyes, he rose and looked at our son for the first time. He looked back at me and said, "Irene is going to love meeting Samuel William."

We had a boy.

A breathing and tiny baby boy.

Within moments, the neonatal team swooped in. They placed Sam on a warming table, where he was surrounded, evaluated, intubated, and hooked up to every monitor possible. Moving quickly, the team wheeled him by my head briefly before heading out to take Sam to the neonatal intensive care unit (NICU), with Peter close behind.

They moved past my bed so quickly I couldn't even see him inside the incubator—just a blur of plastic and doctors' scrubs passing by. All I remember was the fact that he was alive. As the NICU team was wheeling Sam past me and out the door, I caught Dr. Sandhu's eyes and was comforted. There was no panic in his face, and he didn't act rushed. His lack of urgency filled me with hope that Sam was OK.

Later, my mom told me she'd been standing in the hallway outside the OR with Stephanie when the doors burst open and a team of doctors went running by with this tiny little baby in an incubator followed by Peter, who was beaming. As he ran past, he smiled and said, "That's my son! Samuel William." He acted as though he were introducing a full-term baby to the group. He showed no fear or worry, just pride and joy.

With the departure of Sam and his entourage, Dr. Wharton returned his attention to me and began sewing me back up. I lay on that table, my eyes filled with tears of relief. I knew when they left with Sam, he was alive. Now my goal was to get into recovery as quickly as possible so I could see Sam again.

As Dr. Wharton finished sewing me up, the OR was pretty quiet until the phone rang. It was the NICU nurse calling to give me the basic stats on Sam. He was twelve inches long and weighed one pound, twelve ounces. Dr. Wharton stopped mid-stitch. "Can you repeat that?" he asked the OR nurse who had answered the phone.

"They said the baby was twelve inches long and weighed one pound, twelve ounces," she repeated.

"Really. One pound, twelve ounces. Wow. One pound, twelve ounces. That's huge. Great," Dr. Wharton said to no one. He kept mumbling things like "That's so big" and "That's so great" the rest of the time I was on the operating table. I had a hard time wrapping my head around the idea that a one pound, twelve ounce baby was large, but Dr. Wharton's enthusiasm was contagious.

As soon as I was wheeled into recovery, Stephanie and my mom were allowed in. Somehow in Peter's mad dash by everyone, he and Stephanie had arranged how updates would get passed from NICU to recovery. Over the next two and a half hours, Peter was snapping pictures and videos of Sam and texting them to Stephanie. Each time her phone would buzz, the three of us would gather around the little iPhone screen, squeal, and cry. Then Stephanie would text my father, who was still out on his date with Irene. Then she would text her husband, who had to wait downstairs in the hospital as we had too many visitors.

In between phone buzzes, I snoozed. Every part of my body was tired. I was still numb below my epidural site, so I was not able to get out of bed anyway.

In all the excitement and confusion, my dad sent out a birth announcement to a large number of people with Sam's name backwards (William Samuel). TWICE! I guess you could say he was a tad frazzled.

While I lay in that recovery bed, waiting to regain feeling in my legs, I felt an enormous sense of relief and pride. I had done it. I had held onto my son and gotten him as far as I could to give him a chance at life. I knew that the hard work for him was just starting, but for a few fleeting minutes, I let myself relax and enjoy the relief knowing that Sam was alive.

Part Two

The NICU

Chapter 16

My time in the recovery room seemed to take forever. As the hours ticked by, the photos and videos Peter sent me became more of a frustration than a comfort. All I wanted was to get out of that recovery room and up to the NICU for a good long look at Sam.

Before I could be released from the recovery room, I had to regain feeling in my legs and get my pain from the C-section under control. There was also a problem getting me a private room in postpartum. The only room available would have been a shared room with another mom and her newborn baby.

For the second time in my life, hospital staff played the role of protector and refused to put me in that situation. With the perfect room secured, feeling in my legs restored, and enough medication to control my pain, I was released from recovery.

"Released," of course, is a relative term. I was still in my hospital bed, which was now being pushed by a nice transport nurse out of the recovery area and out to the elevator.

This time my ride in the hospital bed felt different. I was no longer in danger of losing my baby. My baby was born, safely tucked away in the NICU, and I was on my way to see him. I was groggy, heavily medicated, exhausted, and exhilarated all at the same time. My glimpse of Sam had been just that—a glimpse.

I didn't get to hold him. I didn't get to touch him. I didn't get a chance to breathe in the newborn baby smell from the top of his head. All I wanted was to get out of my bed and run to the NICU. I would have to settle for a gurney ride.

The elevator doors opened on the fourth floor, and we made our way down the hall toward the NICU. Before my bed was moved into Sam's room, Peter appeared from behind the curtain. He came out to prepare me to meet Sam for the first time. I was instantly annoyed at yet another delay in getting to Sam. I was also jealous. Peter had been with Sam for several hours.

"When you go in there, please try not to be scared," he said gently.

Scared, I thought. *I am not scared.* I just wanted to see Sam.

"OK, can I go in now?" I replied impatiently.

"A few things you need to know. For touching Sam, just put your hand very gently on him, but don't move it around."

"Why not?" I innocently asked.

"His skin is so fragile, movement could tear it," Peter answered.

"Oh," I said quietly as the realization that although Sam was in a safe place, he was far from being out of the woods, hit me full force.

"Also, there will be a lot of alarms that go off. Just tune them out and ignore them."

This would turn out to be some of the best advice I got during Sam's time in the NICU—and something I kept in mind every day for the next ninety-five days. In the beginning, the alarms and bells that measured Sam's vital signs were constant. You could easily drive yourself mad if you didn't shut your mind to them— not that you can block the sounds out completely. I still sometimes hear the bells in my head and have had dreams punctuated by the symphony of NICU alarms.

"OK. Please, can you move so I can go in?" I tried to say nicely, but clearly said with an edge.

With that, Peter moved to the side, and my bed was wheeled next to the warming table Sam was on.

At first, I just stared at the table trying to see Sam, which was next to impossible with all the tubes and wires. His nurse did her best to clear my view, moving his respirator tubes off to the side. My mom, who had been in the recovery room with me, was by my side helping me to remember all the questions I wanted to ask. I was still so groggy, I am not even sure I remembered my own name.

"Are you a little spacey?" my mom asked.

"What?" I replied, clearly spacey.

"Can you see him? What do you think?"

"I see nothing but beauty," I replied, pausing a moment to just stare. "He's beautiful, Mom," I said with tears welling up. What I saw lying on that warming table was the most beautiful sight ever. My son. My beautiful, strong son.

"Oh, Melissa, he's perfect. He's got toes!" my mom said, beaming with pride.

Sitting there next to him in my hospital bed, I gave Sam his first ever mommy lecture:

"You just keep hanging on, strong boy. You come from stubborn stock. You are named after a stubborn, stubborn man and another stubborn, stubborn man. A bunch of stubborn men. It is a big namesake to carry, kiddo. You do those men proud."

With Sam's lecture over, I turned to Mom and said, "He looks better than I thought he would."

Of course, I was totally blinded to the reality laid out in front of me.

Sam was not a perfect little baby. He was a micro-preemie, weighing under one thousand grams. He had waxy, translucent skin that was an unnatural bright red color. He had wires coming out from everywhere. His entire body was covered with long, thick blond hair. His eyes were fused shut. He was only breathing because of the ventilator. He looked more like a newborn kitten crossed with a salamander than a baby.

But I couldn't see any of that. Nor could I see—and yes, I know how crazy this sounds—Sam's fragility or believe any of the dire warnings about how precarious his chances of survival were. Peter knew the survival statistics, but I chose not to learn them until Sam was almost one. I didn't want to know that Sam had only a 40 percent chance of survival, and only a 60 percent chance of leaving the hospital without any major disabilities. Hell, I couldn't even think about possible long-term effects of Sam's prematurity. All I could think about was getting him home. Sam and I were in survival mode, and for me, that meant each day when I entered the NICU, I didn't see anything but my son. I had decided he would survive—he had no other choice.

"Can I touch him?" I asked the nurse.

"Yes, but just gently lay your hand on him. And no movement," she replied.

With permission granted, I reached out and gently laid my palm on his tummy. My hand enveloped him, covering every inch of his body.

"Turn your hand over," his nurse said.

Too tired to question her, I did as told. She lifted Sam's tiny hand and placed it in mine. I beamed. Sam opened his hand and grabbed my finger. Alarms were going off all around me, but I heard none of it. To me, the room was quiet and still, and Sam and I were the only two people there.

"I hate to break this up," my nurse called out, "but it's time to get you to your room."

I had forgotten my nurse was even there with me. I think if she had not spoken up, I would never have left.

"Don't worry, kiddo. I will be back. I love you. Just keep breathing," I called out to Sam as my nurse wheeled my bed out of Sam's room.

Once I was safely tucked in my private room, the nurses left, and just like that, Peter and I were alone for the first time since Sam was born.

The weight of the past few days was in the room with us, but for a few moments, we sat together in my newest hospital bed in silence, holding hands, crying. We had just been through hell together, and now we were parents to this tiny little man. What we were feeling at that moment wasn't fear or sadness but relief and joy.

Chapter 17

The quiet didn't last long. We were soon joined by my post-partum nurse and a hospital-grade breast pump. I stared at her in disbelief.

"Are you kidding?" I asked.

"Sorry?" she replied.

"You want me to pump breast milk? How could I have milk—I wasn't pregnant long enough!"

"You would be surprised what the human body can do. If you pump, the milk will come. And littles like yours need that milk more than anyone." She smiled.

So, less than six hours after giving birth to a micro-preemie, I attached the cones of the pump to my breasts and switched the machine on. In no time, my body showed me how little I knew and started to produce colostrum—not a lot, but enough for me to put in a ten-milliliter bottle about the size of a shotgun bullet, slap on a label, and give to my husband to deliver it to the NICU.

Not that Sam was taking any milk in at this point. It would take a few days before the doctors would call for the introduction of milk into Sam's diet. He was currently getting all his fluids and nutrition from fat emulsion and HA (a vitamin and nutrient supplement), through a tube placed down his throat and into his stomach. Once he was allowed to have breast milk introduced to his feeding tube, he would get less than a milliliter. It would take weeks to build him up to amounts that looked more like a teaspoon of milk.

In the meantime, my milk was being used for "oral care"; a nurse would dip a Q-tip into the milk and rub it on Sam's gums to stimulate his stomach to kick-start his digestive tract. It also protected his gums. A nurse explained to me that regardless of how much milk Sam was taking, it was important for me to get my supply started and established.

With Sam not nursing anytime soon, I realized that the pump and I were going to spend a lot of quality time together. In effect it was going to stand in for Sam until Sam could nurse for himself. I quickly named the pump my "electronic baby" and set alarms on my iPhone to go off every two hours so I would remember to pump—just as if I were feeding a full-term newborn.

This was not how I envisioned bonding with my newborn. Each time the alarm went off, I was reminded how different my situation was. "Nursing" was clinical, done by machine with no connection with my baby. But I was determined to have a strong milk supply. It was the only thing I could actively do to help Sam.

My first night as Sam's mom was anything but restful. Every two hours, my "electronic baby" would cry and I would have to sit up and pump. After pumping, Peter bottled the liquid gold (that's what the nurses called colostrum), labeled it with Sam's NICU label, and walked down the hall to deliver the milk to the freezer. Then he would poke his head in to check on Sam.

I was jealous that he was able to see our boy when I was still too weak to make the trip.

Throughout the night, Peter and my nurses had to constantly remind me that not only had I just had major surgery, but I had been bedbound for the past six days. I had to accept that I was not going to be able to visit Sam until later in the morning.

In reality, I was not planning on going back to the NICU until I could take a proper shower. I smelled so bad it offended me. The last thing I wanted to do was make the kind of first impression that would linger with Sam's doctors and nurses. Even in these trying circumstances, I still had some vanity left.

I had new a goal. Now it was time to formulate a plan. (I do love a good plan.)

Chapter 18

When my morning nurse came in to check my vitals, I asked her about the chances of a shower.

"I am sorry. You have to wait forty-eight hours after surgery to shower," she replied.

"Please. I am disgusting. I have not been able to shower for almost a week. I know I saw you make a face when you entered. You could smell me!" I half joked.

"I'm sorry. Hospital policy. I can get you some dry shampoo if that would help."

I shot her a look that drove her from the room. At this point, I had a thick layer of dry shampoo on my scalp. The absolute last thing I needed was more.

The nurse returned an hour later to see how I was doing.

"I would be doing better if I showered. My head itches. My whole body itches. Please. Please let me shower." This time I was begging.

She smiled and left without a word.

An hour later she was back.

"Please," I pleaded, this time shedding a tear.

"Enough," she said compassionately. "If you promise to wait for a shower chair, and you have two people in there with you, I can't stop you. But I will deny ever telling you this," she said with a smile, and left the room.

The moment the door closed, I called my mom and told her to hurry to the hospital with shampoo, conditioner, soap, face wash, and lotions. My mom, thanks to a massive heart attack and an underlying autoimmune disease, understood how miserable it is to be in the hospital without getting to shower.

Right before my mom arrived, the nurse brought in my shower chair. She didn't say a word, just held her finger to her mouth and said, "Shhhhhhh." As she was about to slip out, my mom arrived, and the nurse decided to give us a hand getting me to the shower. Since I was still weak from being on bed rest, she was worried I might fall.

The first step to getting in the shower was to sit up. We took it slow. First the nurse moved the back of the bed all the way up, putting me in a sitting position.

"How you doing?" Mom asked.

"So far, I'm OK."

Next, with the nurse on one side of me and Peter on the other, I swung my legs over the edge of the bed.

"And now?" Mom asked.

"Still OK," I said.

"Would you tell me if you weren't, Melissa?" Mom asked in that all-knowing mom tone.

"I'm getting that shower," I said. "But I promise I am OK still."

Now came the really big step. I had to stand up and walk. This would be the first time my feet had touched the ground in a week. When it was time to stand, Peter and my nurse gripped my arms a little tighter and helped guide me to a standing position.

My head swam. The room began to spin. I told everyone to wait and give me a minute.

"Do you want to sit back down?" Peter asked timidly.

"Hell no. I just need a moment," I snapped. He didn't understand my need for a shower. He thought I was being vain and careless with my safety.

"OK," I nodded, and we began to move toward the shower. When I say move, I mean more like a very slow shuffle, with breaks every four or five shuffles. It was exhausting. My legs were trembling from all the activity. My incision was throbbing. My head hurt a little. Even still, it was not enough to deter me from the plan of a shower. Nothing was stopping that.

Once we made it to the door to the shower, the nurse and my mom traded positions. She left to get me towels and fresh hospital gowns. While Peter stood behind me holding me up, my mom unsnapped the hospital gown sleeves and let the stale, stinky gown fall to the floor. Then she and Peter lowered me to the shower seat and turned the shower on.

I think I sat in that stream for thirty minutes. I washed everything at least three times. When I finally agreed to get out, my mom helped me dry off with the terrible little hospital towels. She then gently helped put lotion on my legs. My skin soaked it all in. For the first time in a week, my scalp didn't itch and my skin felt normal.

There is no question that that shower will forever rank as the absolute best shower I have ever taken.

Refreshed from my shower, and finally not being offended by my own smell, I was ready to get to the NICU for a visit with my boy. But visiting Sam was no easy task for me. The NICU was on the other side of the hospital floor, way too long for me to walk. The only way I was going to get there was being pushed in a wheelchair. Of course, no ordinary wheelchair would do. The nurse came back with a sparkling purple double-wide. It was as if someone had snuck into the hospital and pimped out the wheelchair—just to give it a little flair.

This time, I remembered the entire trek to the NICU. My mom had to stay behind in my room as only two people were allowed in at a time. Peter pushed my purple chariot down the hall to the elevators where the security guard station was located. We paused there briefly so Peter could introduce me to the security guard. During his trips to the NICU during the night, he had befriended the guard and told him our story. The guard was anxious to meet me. We then turned the corner and rolled down the long hall to the NICU.

This was the first time I really saw the entrance. It was inviting, with "NICU" spelled out in baby blocks above the door. Their pastel colors made the entrance feel warm and welcoming.

The NICU at Alta Bates was not laid out the way I had envisioned it. In my mind, the NICU was going to be this intimidating room with nurses and doctors wearing masks and gowns hustling between isolettes (or incubators) laid out in a long row. I envisioned an impersonal, scary place with no sense of privacy. Quite the opposite was true. This NICU had three different nurseries, which were made up of a central desk where the doctors, nurses, and social workers sat and semi-private rooms surrounding the central desk. Depending on what part of the nursery you were in (and how crowded they were), there would be anywhere from two to four babies in each room. Next to each baby was a glider rocker and a curtain that could be pulled to give a little more privacy. This family-friendly approach went a very long way to making me feel at ease. Also, the lack of masks and gowns on the medical staff helped reduce the intimidation factor.

Just inside the doors was the welcome desk, staffed with two of the kindest people, Allison and Sonia. They greeted us with warm smiles and welcomed us to come inside. They gave us a quick tour, showing us the family room, the only bathroom for parents and family, team meeting rooms, and the overnight room for parents that needed to stay close to their baby for a night or two. In addition, they showed me where the private pumping room was. This room was stocked with pumps and supplies, and had a nice padded glider rocker. They let me know if I preferred, I could always have a pump bedside and pump next to Sam.

The family room was simple but comfortable. There was a table with four chairs, two vinyl lounge chairs, and a small, two-person couch. It would become a place to escape for a quick break or a snack. The hospital was nice enough to stock the refrigerator with yogurts and juices. It was also the only place in the NICU where I would have the opportunity to interact with other families.

After the tour, Peter and I were fitted with our NICU hospital bands—big blue plastic ID bracelets that we would have to wear until Sam was released from the hospital. The bands allowed us access to the hospital and NICU any time of day, and made it so we didn't have to stop at the security desk on the fourth floor to sign in. We would just be able to flash our bands and head in. Of course, my current hospital gown and IV stand were a pretty good indicators that we were not ruffians trying to sneak in.

From there, we were introduced to the art of handwashing— NICU style. Forget everything you ever thought you knew about washing your hands. This was handwashing elevated to an art form. This was no longer a quick stop at the sink. Now we were stopping for a good three minutes, scrubbing with hot water and special hospital-grade soap. We had to make sure to get in between the fingers as well as around the nail bed and under the nails. This was the type of handwashing that left your hands raw and your skin dry and cracked.

I didn't mind. Each time I stopped at the sink and scrubbed, I knew I was doing my part for Sam's well-being. Preemies have such fragile immune systems that handwashing is the number one preventative measure taken by families, visitors, and hospital staff to protect them. Each time we left Sam's room, we had to repeat this process before we could go back in. And not just us, but every single person entering the NICU was required to go through this ritual.

Once our hands were scrubbed clean, Peter finally wheeled me over to Sam's bed in Room 11.

Two women flanked Sam's isolette as we entered the room. Over the next few months, they would become family to me. Laura, or as I like to call her, Auntie Laura, would become Sam's main primary nurse, spending four days a week between 7 a.m. and 3 p.m. taking care of Sam and, by extension, taking care of me. Laura was tall and slender with a wide smile. She was authoritative, kind, and ridiculously funny. The other person was Teresa, a commanding but friendly presence. She was my sensei—the person I turned to with every medical question. During our stay, I looked for Teresa the moment I arrived to get the medical report on how Sam was doing.

Once the introductions were over, Teresa filled us in on Sam's status.

"So, Sam is a champ," Teresa started. "He had a great night, and all his vitals are stable this morning."

"Thank God," I said, breathing a huge sigh of relief.

"I am really encouraged by the state of his lungs," Teresa continued. "He is breathing over the ventilator most of the time, so we have turned the settings down with the hope of taking him off the vent soon."

"Wow. I guess the temper tantrum I threw in Labor & Delivery to get the steroids paid off." I smiled.

"Why don't you settle in and talk to Sam. He is used to your voices, so hearing them will let him know you are with him," Teresa suggested.

As she was leaving the room, she added, "Stay as long as you want. This is your room and your baby."

I would have stayed forever, but after a short time my exhaustion kicked in and the electronic baby was calling, so Peter wheeled me back to my room.

The rest of the afternoon, I rested, pumped, and mentally prepared myself for telling Irene about her brother.

After Peter left to go pick up Irene from kindergarten and bring her back to the hospital, I imagined the ideal scene of what was about to unfold: Peter and Irene arrive at the hospital. Irene and I hug. We tell her that her baby brother has been born and that he is very little and sick. In my mind, Irene would be curled up in my lap or lying in bed with me through all of this. I would be holding her, and comforting her when she talked about how scared she was. Then we would show her some pictures and talk her through everything she was seeing. If, after that, she wanted to meet him, we would bring her to the NICU.

That was my vision.

The reality was much different.

By the time Irene arrived, Peter had already told her she was now an official big sister. I didn't have time to be disappointed that I was cut out of that moment, as Irene was wound up and excited.

"Can I meet him?" Irene asked the moment she got into my room.

"Can I have a hug first please?" I asked with a smile.

Irene laughed. "Of course, Mama!"

She bounded from the door to where I was sitting. Her hug was a little too hard, but I didn't care. Irene's arms around me felt safe and warm. I let out a big cleansing breath and said, "Before you go meet Sam, there are some things we need to tell you."

"Fine," Irene whined.

I pulled out the iPad with all the pictures on it and started to scroll through them.

"Before you meet Sam, we have to stop at the desk and introduce you to Sonia. Then we have to wash your hands really good."

"Dad already told me all this. Can we go now?" Irene was clearly running out of patience.

"Not yet. I want to show you a picture of Sam's room and a few pictures of him. He doesn't look like a normal baby, and I don't want you to be scared."

Irene sighed.

She breezed through the photos, smiling at each one, and again told us to take her to her brother. Still not convinced Irene understood what she was about to see, I pulled out one of the diapers Sam's nurse had given us to show Irene. She took one look at the tiny diaper, burst out laughing, and said, "Mommy, this is smaller than my dolly's diaper!"

"As small as that diaper is, it's still too big for your brother," Peter added.

Her eyes got really big, and she looked at me and said, "Wow. I have got to see that!"

In hindsight, I realize I was the one who was scared. I desperately needed to hold one of my children in my arms and feel the normalcy of being a mom. But Irene was having none of it. She was too excited.

It became obvious that we were not going to deter her, so off to the NICU we went. Peter was pushing my wheelchair with Irene curled up in my lap. Luckily, I was hopped up on enough painkillers that the weight of her body didn't hurt; instead, it felt like home. At least that part of my vision of Irene meeting her brother had come true!

We arrived in Sam's room, and Irene looked at Laura and said, "I'm the big sister," then asked if she could touch Sam. Laura smiled and told her that she could talk to Sam, but that, for now, touching him wasn't possible.

We opened the door to his isolette just a little so Irene could share some sisterly words of love with her brother.

"Hi! I'm Irene. I'm your big sister!" Irene looked back at me to make sure it was OK. I nodded for her to continue.

"I want you to come home soon so we can play together. Oh! Did you know we have three cats? They like to sleep in your crib." Irene giggled.

Both Peter and I stood there, stunned by the maturity Irene was showing. The whole scene was sweet and perfect. We did our best to just let this be Irene's time with Sam. We watched her. We tried to hide our tears. We smiled.

We stayed as a family in Room 11 for about thirty minutes. Finally, the electronic baby cried, and we all headed back to my room for Jell-O and a good pumping session.

Chapter 19

An hour or so after Peter and Irene left, my hospital-assigned social worker, Misty, came by to introduce herself.

"Why do I need a social worker?" I asked cautiously. In my mind social workers were for babies who needed protection from their parents.

"I'm here to help you navigate the hospital, teach you the ins and outs of life in the NICU, help with your insurance, and make sure you are being taken care of," Misty replied.

It was a good answer. I liked how she didn't take offense to my question.

"Do you need anything? Do you have any questions for me?"

"I don't even know where to start."

"Let's start with parking. These parking passes are gold around here. It will allow your husband to park for free in the lot."

It would take a few days for me to realize how valuable those passes were. The hospital parking lot would have bankrupted us.

We talked for a little while about the NICU and how to be an advocate for Sam. Just as she was about to go and let me rest, I realized I had one question for her.

"I had trouble nursing with my first child. My milk dried up really early on. Is there someone I can talk to here to make sure that doesn't happen this time?"

"Of course. I will make sure our lactation consultant comes and talks to you before the day is done."

Once Misty left, I found myself in a suddenly unfamiliar situation —all alone. The silence and privacy were great at first. It had been a few days since I was alone, and I am a person who really values my "me time." Now here I was. After taking a deep breath, the stillness suddenly became overwhelming. My mind began to drift to some dark places, and I was overcome with a jumble of emotions I had bottled up in the past seven days. Fear, joy, terror, pain, hope, and isolation were just a few of the emotions I was experiencing. So much had happened to me. I mean, one Friday I came home from work, and the following Friday I was sitting in my hospital room, mom to a one pound, twelve ounce baby.

I had to find an outlet for everything that was rattling around in my head.

Out of nowhere, I was hit with the idea that I should start to write. I had never kept a journal before, but for some reason, I just knew that writing was going to be my salvation. I would write every day about Sam, his progress, and my angst associated with his progress. This would be my therapy—a place for me to put all my emotions so they would not consume me. I would also put my writings out there as a way for my friends and family to keep up on how things were going.

Having made that decision, I started a blog. The emotional release from that first entry was wonderful. I wept with each word I wrote. I poured everything I had been holding back into those words, and with the push of a button I distributed it for the world (or at least my friends and family) to see. When I was done, I looked around my quiet room and took a moment. I realized that just by writing down everything I was thinking and feeling, I felt freed from my thoughts and emotions. They were not rattling around in my head anymore; instead, they were trapped on "paper" and no longer bogging me down.

Over the weeks and months to come, my writing would become the best way for me to connect to my friends and family and to keep them connected to me. Writing about Sam's status and mine would keep them up to speed on how he was doing and, though I didn't intend for this to happen, create a feedback loop between us. I would find that my writings opened me up to people I had not seen or spoken to in years—and in some cases, ever. Despite being physically alone, I was more connected than ever to people.

Sometime in the middle of my second night in the hospital, I spiked a high fever and had to be put back on an IV so I could be pumped full of fluids and antibiotics. My doctors were concerned that I had developed a post-operative infection. It would not be the first time. After I lost the twin pregnancy, I had a pretty severe uterine infection, which caused heavy bleeding for more than a month. Because of this, the doctors were going to be extra cautious with me.

The nurses drew about five vials of blood and ordered me to limit my visits to the NICU to just twice a day. In some ways, I was OK with that. Between the fever and the shakes, I was having a hard time, and my energy level was near rock bottom. I was relieved to be staying in my room, napping and pumping. My parents and Peter would alternate between entertaining me, Irene, and Sam throughout the day.

Sam, on the other hand, was having a great second night in the NICU. He was doing well for a baby his gestational age and size. Because of all the blood tests Sam had to have, the doctors ordered a blood transfusion to increase his blood count. When you are less than one thousand grams, your body does not have a lot of blood in it to begin with. Each time the nurses drew blood, his body couldn't regenerate the blood fast enough.

The idea of Sam getting a blood transfusion scared me. It felt invasive for such a small and fragile baby. I decided to make one of my trips to the NICU to see Sam and talk to someone before the transfusion began.

I arrived in his room just as Teresa was finishing a blood draw from Sam's foot.

"I can see the panic all over your face," Teresa said. "I promise, this is totally normal."

"How can taking that much blood from someone so tiny be normal?" I asked.

"I do this all day, every day. I promise you, this is not something to fear. Your baby has been through a lot in the past three days. He just needs a boost of blood to help increase his blood pressure and stabilize his heart rate."

"Well, I'm not leaving till it's done."

That lasted about ten minutes; then I started to have chills and Peter insisted on taking me back to my room. At least Sam responded really well to the blood transfusion.

At the end of Sam's second full day in the NICU, Dr. Sandhu came to visit me. I remembered Dr. Sandhu from the delivery room and was really glad to see him. We spent the next hour discussing Sam's treatment plan and prognosis.

"Your son is showing us that he is very strong," Dr. Sandhu started. "He has improved daily, and we think by tomorrow we will be able to take him off the ventilator."

The world stopped. I was sure I had misheard Dr. Sandhu.

"I'm sorry. Can you repeat that? You are taking him off the ventilator?" I asked.

"If nothing changes tonight, I will have the ventilator removed and place Sam on the high-flow cannula."

I just stared at him.

"It is important for you to know that this may only be temporary. His lungs may not be strong enough, so it's possible we will have to put him back on the ventilator."

At this point, half of me thought Dr. Sandhu was crazy and should look at increasing his malpractice insurance, while the other half was screaming, "Woo-hoo!"

Either way, with Sam off the ventilator, Dr. Sandhu told me that I could hold my little man if I wanted.

"If I want?" I half shouted and half asked. "Of course I want to!"

"Good. I have seen the best improvements in these little ones once we get them into their parents' arms," Dr. Sandhu said.

"My arms are ready! What time should I be there?"

Dr. Sandhu smiled. "If everything goes well, tomorrow morning you can hold him."

That night was a restless one for me. I was feeling better and my fever had finally broken, but I could not sleep. I kept closing my eyes, drifting, and waking up with a start, convinced that it was morning and time for me to head to the NICU to hold Sam. Of course, only five minutes or so had passed each time I did this.

I continued this game until morning. Finally, at 9 a.m., I couldn't take it anymore, and I slowly made my way to the NICU.

I was healed enough that I could walk the halls of the hospital on my own. Walking was part of recovery, but that didn't mean it felt good. I was careful to move slowly and to hold onto the wall as I went.

When I got there, Sam was still on the ventilator.

"Shit."

"Excuse me?" his nurse responded.

"Sorry! I thought he would be off the vent by now so I could hold him," I replied.

She laughed. "No, we are going to extubate him at one p.m."

"Oh." I'm sure the defeat was painted all over my face.

"Don't worry. It will happen today. Come back after one p.m. and you will hold him."

I believed her. I wasn't sure I liked her at the moment, but I believed her.

I called Peter to let him know my date with Sam was delayed. Then I headed back to my room to watch the clock and wait.

To help the time pass, I agreed to let some people visit me. I had been holding off on nonfamily visitors, but my friend Christian's visit brought a huge smile to my face. Christian is a larger-than-life individual who has never ceased to be there for me—no matter the crisis or celebration—ever since the day we met at orientation at Barnard College. She also has an uncanny ability to know the perfect thing to bring to lighten the mood.

On this occasion, she arrived with a huge box of the most beautiful cupcakes I had ever seen. Each one was covered in elaborate gum paste flowers and butterflies. Just as I was reaching in the box to sample one of the treats, she swatted my hand away.

"Those aren't for you!" she admonished.

"Why not? I want a cupcake," I pleaded with as much self-pity as I could muster.

"Those are for Sam's nurses. I even made you a sign to go with them, so they know who brought them."

I just smiled. Of course Christian had thought to bring cupcakes for the nurses so they would know our family would treat them as well as we needed them to treat our son.

That didn't mean I wasn't frustrated she hadn't thought to bring one extra for me to eat, of course.

Christian left after a couple of hours, and as I waited for my chance to hold Sam, the idea of having other people keep me company increasingly seemed like a good one. Peter was having a morning date with Irene, so he was occupied. My parents were taking Irene for the afternoon, so they needed the morning to get errands done. Lucky for me, my aunt Emilie was in town from Los Angeles visiting her daughters and their families. Emilie and two of my cousins, Carol and Jennifer, really wanted to visit.

They were lifesavers, as I had never seen a clock tick so slowly as it had that morning. The second hand seemed frozen, making each minute take forever. I would have gone crazy waiting if it had not been for the visit. The three of them talked my ear off—in a good way. The huge supply of See's Candy Nuts and Chews, our grandmother's favorite, they brought didn't hurt either.

Peter made it to the hospital around 12:30, which was perfect, as I needed to pump and my aunt and cousins were ready to head out. Once they left, Peter turned to me, his arms folded, his brow furrowed . . . He did not look happy.

"Seriously, Melissa."

I sensed I was in trouble, but I had no idea why.

"Um . . ." I mumbled.

"Seriously. You were going to hold our son for the first time without me there?"

"Seriously?" he repeated.

Yikes. It hadn't even occurred to me that Peter might want to be there when I held Sam for the first time. I felt like I was a bad wife for not considering his feelings. My groveling and apologizing took up the next thirty minutes—which was good, because by the time he accepted my apology, it was time to head to the NICU to get my hands on Sam.

This time when we arrived the nurse was smiling at us.

"He has been off the vent for about an hour now and is doing great!"

I pulled back the quilt covering his isolette and burst into tears. It hadn't occurred to me that with the ventilator tube out of his mouth, I would be able to see his face. His lips looked just like his daddy's. His chin was beautiful and perfect. The jury on his nose was still out as the cannula covered it, but I was convinced that would be perfect too.

"Does this mean I get to hold him?" I asked nervously.

"Only if you want to," the nurse replied.

"God yes. Now what?"

"Sit down in the rocker, and I will bring him to you."

I settled into the chair. Peter moved off to the side, ensuring he was in the best photo-taking spot. The nurse put a pillow in my lap to help support my arms.

"Before I bring him to you, a few rules."

"Of course. There had to be rules," I said, trying to hide my impatience.

"First. Once I place Sam on your chest, I need you to keep your movements to a minimum."

"OK."

"Second. You need to keep your voice down. Loud sounds can startle him, which can disrupt his breathing."

This was a new one—but I was not going to argue. "OK," I said a little more impatiently.

"Third. Babies of this size can normally only tolerate being held for thirty to forty-five minutes, if that."

"Got it," I snapped.

She then listed a bunch of other things to be aware of and look for, but they all sounded like "blah, blah, blah, blah, blah."

I was done waiting. I was done listening. I wanted to hold my boy.

"I promise that I have heard everything. I understand. Please, let me hold my son," I pleaded.

A second nurse arrived to help move all the tubes and wires. The main nurse opened the side of the isolette and in a choreographed dance lifted Sam and placed him right in the middle of my chest.

I looked down onto my beautiful little boy's face while feeling his warmth against me. He was so small and fragile, yet as I held him, I saw none of that. All I saw was my son. I stared at him with tears of joy streaming down my face. He was so precious, so beautiful, and all mine. Well . . . OK, mine, and Peter's, and Irene's, and my parents' . . .

I don't think I moved the entire time I was holding him—partially paralyzed by his fragility and partially paralyzed by the joy of the moment.

There is one picture from that first cuddle that is among my favorites ever taken of Sam and me. I love the awe on my face as I gaze upon my son, drawn into the perfection of his face. This is the picture I always showed people when they asked to see what Sam looked like at birth. I would pull out my phone and beam as I turned the screen around to show this most special moment. It wasn't until months later, when my brother, who was now living in Lesotho, was visiting, that I stopped to look more closely at the picture. We were in front of the computer, looking at images from Sam's NICU stay, when we got to this one.

"That's the one," Brian said.

"Yeah. I love this one too," I innocently replied.

"Oh no," said Brian. "I hate this picture."

"Huh?" I said, turning toward him.

"This is the picture that drove me to finish all the tequila in my house."

I looked back at the picture and for the first time I saw that this wasn't just a beautiful mother and child image. This was an image of a clueless woman holding a tiny baby in her hands. Sam's face was the size of my thumb to the first knuckle. His skin was bright red. His eyes were fused shut. Seeing that image through my brother's eyes was mind-blowing. My mind had protected me from all of this by allowing me to only see the beauty in the image. Thank God for that. I told all of this to Brian. He smiled and told me he was glad I had been oblivious, as it had obviously allowed me to stay strong.

That first cuddle session with Sam was a wonderful experience for me. Despite all the warnings that Sam might not respond well to being out of the isolette and that he might last only forty-five minutes, he lasted an hour and forty-five minutes in my arms, and probably could have lasted longer, but my electronic baby was crying and I was more than ready to answer the call. Having Sam on my chest activated my milk-producing glands, and I felt my milk let down four times during our cuddle.

"I hate to do this, but if I don't go pump, I am afraid I will explode," I said, breaking the silence in the room.

"Excuse me?" the nurse responded.

"I am ready to put Sam back."

Once again, the two nurses in a choreographed dance of baby and wire moving lifted Sam up off my chest and gently placed him back in his isolette.

The euphoria of holding Sam carried me through the rest of the day.

Chapter 20

Later that evening, my doctor told me I was cleared for discharge the next day. I had already spent nine long days at the hospital, making my tenth day my last as a patient. This news was exciting and terrifying at the same time. My body was healing nicely, and, physically, I was ready. I was also overjoyed with the thought of sleeping in my own bed, wearing clothing that didn't open in the back, and having a refrigerator I could go to anytime to grab something to eat. More than that, I was going to finally be there for Irene when she got home from school and could cuddle with her whenever I wanted.

On the other hand, I would be leaving Sam behind. I knew he was in the best possible place for such a little man. He had the best nurses, the best care, the best of everything. But he would no longer have his mama down the hall.

I had a restless night, and once morning came I made a vow to make the most of my last day in the hospital, spending as much time as I could with Sam, talking with his doctors, meeting with my social worker, Misty, and talking with the lactation consultant, Deborah.

Obviously, spending time with Sam was vital, but my top priority was talking with Deborah. I felt like I had failed Sam on so many levels at this point, there was no way I was going to let my milk supply fail him as well. With Irene, my milk supply began to dry up when she was just three months old and we had to start supplementing with formula. By the time Irene was six months old, my milk was totally gone, and Irene was 100 percent formula fed. It was disheartening for me not to breastfeed Irene as long as I had planned. I was more than determined not to have this happen with Sam.

I knew how important it was that Sam get breast milk. While breast milk is important for full-term babies, it is critical for preemies, as it helps boost the immune system and protects them from necrotizing enterocolitis (NEC), a dangerous disease where the bacteria living in the intestines begin to attack the intestinal wall, which can lead to the intestines dying and then a hole forming in the bowels. Producing breast milk was the one thing I could still do for Sam at this point.

Not that the pumping was all positive for me. Yes, I was getting a good amount of milk out so far. But I had developed huge blisters on my nipples, and one of my nipples had started to bleed. When I asked the nurses for a breast pad to protect my poor nipples, they had nothing. Luckily, my nurse pulled a MacGyver. She cut a maxi pad in half and taped one half to each breast. Nothing says sexy like a hospital gown + Percocet sweats + maxi pads on the boobs.

None of that was going to deter me, though. I was desperate to talk with the lactation consultant to get guidance on how to set myself up for milk success.

Deborah was so encouraging.

"You are already doing a great job," she told me.

"But how can I make sure my supply doesn't dry up?"

"Keep doing what you are doing. Pump every two hours. Pump next to Sam's bed," she suggested.

"I can do that. I can. But what about after I am released? What do I do at night?"

"Look at pictures or videos of Sam while you pump," she suggested. "Oh, and drink lots and lots of water."

Just as Deborah was about to leave, she turned back and gave me one last piece of advice.

"Melissa, the best way to keep your supply going is not to stress over it. Don't worry. Your body is built for this, just have faith."

I was only four days in with a baby and my supply was coming in nicely, so there was no reason to think it wouldn't stay that way. Just as I had to believe everything with Sam was going to be OK, I had to take a leap of faith and believe if I kept pumping, my milk supply would not let me down.

After talking with Deborah, I headed down to the NICU to see and hold Sam. This time, the nurse set us up to do a skin-to-skin hold (also known as a kangaroo hold), where Sam was placed directly on my chest with nothing between us. The second he got there, he reached out his little hand and started to rub my chest. I turned into a big pile of mush—tears pouring down my face, which of course led to snot dripping out of my nose.

As we neared the end of daylight, I was finally discharged from the hospital. I wish I could tell you I was the epitome of stoicism when we pulled away, but that would be a lie. I think I started bawling in the elevator and cried the whole way home. I just wanted to tuck Sam under my arm and bring him with me.

When we walked in the front door of our house, the cats and my parents were waiting for us with Irene. One look at the mass of blond curls bouncing around my little girl's face and all of the regret about leaving the hospital just melted away, at least for a moment. Sitting with her on our couch and snuggling made me feel better. I knew coming home was the right thing to do, and the smile on Irene's face confirmed it for me.

My parents had been kind enough to bring a Chinese food feast over, so we all sat down at the kitchen table for family dinner. The meal had all the components I had been missing while in the hospital: a chair, a table, good food and family. It was so simple and so rewarding. With each bite of food, I felt closer and closer to normal.

After dinner, my parents said goodnight and left the three of us to enjoy our first night together in ten days.

Irene made the most of my return.

"Daddy, you go now. Mom and I are going to play," Irene demanded.

Peter looked a little dejected but did as he was ordered.

"String bean," I said, using one of my favorite nicknames for Irene, "I am pretty tired. How about we go down to your room, pick a good book to read, and cuddle?"

"OK!" Irene jumped off the couch and ran down to my room. "I'm waiting, Mama," she called up the stairs.

"I'm coming. I'm just slower than you."

Despite the calls of the electronic baby and the pain in my abdomen from the C-section, I crawled into Irene's bed, pushed the hundreds of stuffed animals to the floor, wrapped my arms around her, and smothered her with kisses. I breathed her in, burying my face in her hair.

For the next hour, Irene and I stayed in her bed talking about her third week of kindergarten and how it went. I had missed so much, and I was not going to miss another second.

"Ladies, I hate to break this up, but it is a school night and way past Irene's bedtime," Peter called from outside the door.

"I promise, when you wake up in the morning, I will be here, kiddo," I reassured Irene as I gingerly got up from her bed.

"When I wake up, I am going straight to your room to get in your bed," Irene said as she pulled me down for a kiss.

I pulled the pink satin comforter up to her chin and said, "You better. I love you. So, so much."

It was such a simple thing, but after ten days of not being there for her, it felt so good and normal to just be a part of her bedtime routine again.

A quick session with the electronic baby and I finally got to slide into my own bed.

Oh. My. God.

After ten days in hospital beds with plastic-covered hospital mattresses and threadbare sheets that never stayed in place, our bed felt like heaven. Our mattress was firm and plush at the same time. And the sheets—oh, the sheets! These were not some fifty-thread-count hospital sheets. These were two-hundred-thread-count Target specials. I had not really appreciated our bed until that moment.

Despite the comfort level, I was unable to sleep. Sam was not right down the hallway. My anxiety started to build, and I could not shake the feeling that something was going wrong. It wasn't rational. Even when I was in the hospital, Sam was not next to me. But now Sam was six whole miles away. For a person recovering from major abdominal surgery and on a driving ban, this distance felt insurmountable.

I began crying uncontrollably—so much that I was hyperventilating. My weeping and gasping for air woke Peter. The moment I saw the whites of his eyes, I croaked, "You have to go to the hospital to check on Sam."

"Why, did they call? Is something wrong?" Peter responded, clearing the sleep from his eyes.

"No," I cried. "I just need eyes on him. I can't drive, and we can't leave Irene alone. You have to go. I need you to go." My voice was rising and shaking. "Please. I need to know he is OK. Please."

By this time, Peter was already out of bed, slipping pants on and looking for his keys. "OK. OK. Try to calm down. I am going. I will text you the moment I get there," Peter said as he walked out the bedroom door.

He was more than happy to oblige. Not only did it mean he could escape the crazy emotional mess that was his wife, it also meant he would have some alone time with his son. Not that Peter had worked up the nerve to hold Sam yet—it was enough for him just to put a hand on his chest.

The eleven minutes from the time Peter left our house to when the first picture arrived were rough. Being left alone wasn't the best thing for me. I had nobody to talk me off the crazy train I was trying to board.

Luckily, that first image along with the words "He's doing great" calmed me down. Peter spent about twenty minutes with Sam, sending me one photo after another until I was finally calm and secure enough to settle into my wonderful bed and sleep for a glorious two straight hours, when the electronic baby cried and the pumping began.

The next morning, Irene came bounding into our room. She took one look at me half asleep in the bed and screamed, "Mama! You're here. It wasn't a dream!" and then catapulted herself into the bed. Had it not been for the pain from my C-section incision, this would have been a perfect way to start the day. Once I could breathe again, I wrapped my arms around Irene and nuzzled into her hair.

"Irene. Unless you are going to school in your pajamas, it's time to get dressed," Peter said, breaking up the love fest.

Irene just clung to me. And I clung to her. I missed Irene's hugs. I missed the smell of her hair. And I desperately needed to hold one of my children in my arms. After another five minutes, Irene and I reached a compromise.

"How about if I go with you and help you pick out an outfit?" I asked.

"OK, Mama," Irene said, taking my hand and helping me get up.

We walked to her room, holding hands, and looked for the best pink outfit we could find.

"Will you be here when I get home today?" Irene asked.

"Nope," I said.

"Oh. But I want you here, Mama."

"Honey, I will be in the car to pick you up from school instead," I said with a big smile.

"You will!" Irene screamed as she lunged in for a hug.

"I love you, kiddo. I can't wait to hear all about your day. Be good at school, OK?"

"I will, Mama. I promise."

As soon as Peter and Irene left, I grabbed the phone to call the NICU and check in on Sam. It had been a whole five hours since I last called the hospital.

It turned out those five hours had been pretty exciting. Sam had suffered a number of bradycardia (or brady) and apnea events.

Sometimes preemies forget to take a breath. They are so young, and their lungs are extremely immature, it just slips their mind that breathing is a good idea. So, apnea occurs when there is a pause in breathing that lasts more than twenty seconds. A brady happens when their heart rate dips below eighty beats per minute. Apnea often causes a brady to happen, as well as a desaturation, when the oxygen level falls below eighty-five. The doctors hoped that Sam would self-correct when he had a brady and his heartbeat would return to normal. In instances where he didn't self-correct, the nurses stimulated him either by tapping his feet or, as he got older, by vigorously rubbing his back or even shaking him. As a preventative measure, Teresa started Sam on caffeine. Just like in adults, caffeine in babies can help raise their heart rate. The nurses assured me they were giving him Peet's coffee, a local brand, and not Starbucks. I could always count on them to lighten the heavy moments.

After hearing about Sam's rough night, the moment Peter got back from taking Irene to school, I demanded to be taken to the hospital. I needed to see Sam and I hoped to hold him. Luckily, Peter was out on paternity leave for the next few weeks from his job at a mobile game company, so he was able to be my on-demand chauffeur.

Walking into his room, I immediately felt better. Just seeing Sam breathing was enough to put me at ease. I broached the idea of maybe getting a cuddle in, but Sam's nurse that day gently suggested that I skip it—for his sake. I tried not to let the disappointment overtake me. I wanted to hold him, but not if it was unsafe for Sam.

Teresa came in soon after to talk with us.

"So, I hear Sam had a rough night," Teresa began. "I want you to take a deep breath and realize that this is going to happen. A lot. A's and B's are just part of life in the NICU."

"A's and B's?" I asked.

"Apneas and bradys. So common, we gave them shorter names," she joked.

Some days Sam would have one event, and other days he would have so many, I lost count. The main thing I learned was to stay calm. I never did get used to the A's and B's, but I did my best to be comfortable with them.

We spent a few hours with Sam, and then Peter took me

home to rest. Irene's first ever back-to-school night was that evening. I had already missed two weeks of kindergarten—there was no way I was going to miss meeting her teacher and seeing her classroom.

I rested all afternoon until it was time to go pick up Irene at school. I had promised her I would be in the car, and I was not going to break my promise. She bounded down the stairs and lit up when she saw me. We came home to a nice dinner of homemade lasagna that had been left on our front porch by one of my friends. My parents came over to watch Irene, and off we went to Irene's school—just like normal parents of a kindergartner.

Walking into the auditorium was a total sensory overload. The past eleven days I had been surrounded by noises, but these were hospital noises: PA systems, alarms, beeps, drips, and the litany of other sounds you hear in a hospital. This was different. This was an auditorium filled with parents, all talking at once. Before I even had a chance to acclimate myself, people started to notice me. I imagined what they were thinking: "Oh, she's the one," or "Those poor people," or "How could they be here with everything they are going through?" One after another, moms and dads of Irene's classmates approached me. Each one meant well. They all just wanted to let me know they were thinking about me. Each one wanted to know how Sam was doing.

Unfortunately, every time someone approached, I could feel the lump in my throat get bigger. Their kindness hurt, and their sympathy overwhelmed me. I quickly excused myself from the auditorium and found a chair in the hallway. I was alone out there for a few minutes, which was good, as it allowed me time and space to cry. Soon the overflow crowd filled the hallway, and the looks I got from parents that didn't know me were pretty telling.

This time I imagined they were saying, "What the hell is wrong with her?"

Peter came out of the main auditorium to find me. "This is too much. Let's go home," he suggested.

"No. Just give me a few minutes. I am not leaving," I snapped at him.

"Melissa, please. It's clear this is too much for you."

"Stop. I am not missing this. I can't miss this." I dug in my heels. I had made it this far, and I really wanted to go to Irene's classroom.

We were the first to arrive in the classroom. Irene's teacher, Mr. Thompson, was caught off guard by our presence. After a brief moment of silence, Mr. Thompson approached us, wrapped his arm around me, gave me a pat on the back, and with a knowing nod, stood next to me until people started to arrive. I was overwhelmed with the knowledge that Mr. Thompson had provided Irene with the same stability and support. I found a chair in the back of the room and alternated between listening to what was being said and drifting off, crying the entire time, of course. By the end of the evening, I was emotionally and physically exhausted but glad I had stuck to my guns—for myself and for Irene.

Chapter 21

Sensing my need for some girl time, the next day Peter dropped Irene off at school and called Stephanie. He let her know that I was in need of a girly intervention—and boy, was he right.

I hadn't seen Stephanie since the night Sam was born. Between her two kids and her job, it had been too hard for her to get away. But, just as we had been there for each other our whole lives, as soon as Peter told her I needed her, she dropped everything and rushed over.

As usual, Stephanie knew just what I needed. Aside from arriving with a dozen donuts from the best shop in the East Bay, Stephanie brought our mutual friend Lisa along to give me a manicure. In a moment of vain weakness, I had gotten gels for the first time in my life while I was pregnant. The gels had held up until I began the vigorous NICU handwashing routine. By the time Stephanie and Lisa showed up on my doorstep, my beautiful nails looked like something out of a horror movie. It was time to get the gel off and go back to my natural nails.

And suddenly there we were: three girlfriends, chatting over donuts and a manicure—talking about everything we could that was NOT related to my premature baby.

"Wait," I called out, trying to catch my breath from laughing. "Are you telling me the dog ate three baby socks?"

"Yep. He pooped them out two days later," Steph responded.

"I thought Swiss mountain dogs were supposed to be smart," Lisa said.

"You've met Owen. You really thought he was smart?" Steph was laughing so hard it was contagious.

Anyone passing by would have thought we were just three ladies having a laugh, except I was in pajamas, doped up on pain-killers, and pausing our conversation at the two-hour mark to pump milk for my newborn, who was nowhere to be seen. Either way, the visit was exactly the right dose of normal mixed with friendly support, which then gave me the space I needed to reset my emotions.

Once Stephanie left, Peter and I headed to the NICU for a visit with Sam. We got there at a shift change, so we waited.

Teresa saw us in the hallway and approached us. She asked to talk. I felt the bottom of my stomach drop. I didn't think being approached by the nurse practitioner upon arrival could be good news.

"Don't panic," she started, "however, Sam's chest X-rays were showing a little fluid around his lungs."

"OK," I hesitantly added.

"We have taken Sam off the high-flow cannula and moved him to SiPAP."

"What the hell is SiPAP?" I asked.

"It's a step between the cannula and the ventilator. Air is forced at two levels of pressure into Sam's lungs via a mask." Before I even had time to react, Teresa added, "Sam has responded well to SiPAP, and just had a near-perfect X-ray."

"So, I should stop the mild panic that is starting?" I asked.

"Yes. But there is more. Well, more to help you stop panicking."

Peter and I exchanged a glance.

"Sam had his first head ultrasound today to check for brain bleeds."

We had been warned that aside from NEC, brain bleeds were very common in preemies and could lead to a number of issues, including cerebral palsy and brain injury.

"Please tell me it was OK."

"It was perfect. The only thing we saw was a brain." Teresa smiled.

This was a big hurdle we needed to get past. I knew better than to think that he was in the clear, but this result brought a huge sense of relief. The next brain scan would not be for another month.

That is where our good visit ended. The afternoon nurse assigned to Sam was just not a good fit for us. She was a humorless, condescending, mean bitch. Peter left the room soon after arriving. There was no place for him to sit—and this nurse was not making things comfortable. Once he left, the nurse turned to me.

"How long are you planning on being here?" she snapped at me.

"As long as I can," I replied, my defenses on high alert.

"Well, if you were hoping to hold him, I wouldn't," she told me.

"And why is that?" I asked. This was the first time anyone had been less than welcoming with me.

As opposed to answering my question, the nurse just let out an annoyed sigh and started to fill out some paperwork or something.

"Since you don't have a reason, I am here to hold MY son," I told her defiantly.

Another huge sigh. "If you insist, sit down and I will bring him to you."

Five minutes after she placed Sam on my chest, he had a really bad brady.

"You're holding him wrong!" she snapped at me. "I told you this was a bad idea. He needs to go back."

At this point, I was in tears. A nurse had just accused me of causing a brady and did nothing to help me correct whatever it was I was doing wrong. I felt like a nuisance and a failure. It was so stressful. Sam was even able to pick up on my stress, as he began to squirm on my chest and have brady after brady. It was clear that this cuddle session was a failure.

"Fine. Put him back," I cried.

She looked at me and without a word took Sam and put him back in his isolette.

On my way out of Sam's room, I ran into Misty, who could see how upset and stressed I looked.

"Whoa. What happened? Is Sam OK?" Misty asked.

"I don't know. That nurse, she was just awful."

"Don't leave. Just give me a second," Misty said as she headed into Sam's room. A moment later she was back. "I just wanted to make sure he was OK. He is."

"That nurse was just so mean and condescending. She upset me so much that I think I upset Sam."

"I'm so sorry. Would you like to make sure she is not assigned to Sam's case again?"

"I can ask for that?"

"Yep. Say the word, and I will make sure you never have to deal with her again."

"Please. I do not want to see 'Evil Nurse' near my son or me again."

"Consider it done." Misty smiled.

On our way home, we went by Irene's school to pick her up. Irene took one look at my tear-streaked face and said, "Don't cry, Mama. It's going to be OK."

I gave her a weak smile. "I know, baby."

She reached into her backpack and pulled out a colorful

plastic heart she had made from beads. "It's for Sam!" she said, smiling.

If that wasn't heartwarming enough, when we got home, Irene ran to her room and grabbed her new Minnie Mouse doll. "You can sleep with her tonight, Mama, since you can't sleep with Sam."

Her thoughtfulness and maturity overwhelmed me. After feeling like I was a failure as a parent in our visit to the NICU, Irene reminded me that I was doing some things right.

Chapter 22

During this period, both when I was in the hospital and when I was newly released, my friends, despite being supportive, did not really understand what I was going through. It was hard to lean on them. They were eager to help, but they didn't understand there wasn't anything they could do. Often, people turn to clichés when they don't know what else to say. But I found those statements more hurtful than saying nothing at all.

When someone said, "I can't imagine how hard this must be for you!" all I heard was: "I am so glad I am not you!" An innocent question of "How did this happen?" sounded like "How could you have screwed up this badly?" The worst was "These things happen for a reason." What possible reason could there be? I failed at gestating? Sam failed at gestating? I had done something horrible in a past life and was now being punished for it?

I knew people meant well, but my already fragile psyche couldn't take it. Making new friends in the NICU was also difficult, as people were laser-focused on their own children and their own woes. Parents who had just entered the NICU world were too shell-shocked to see anyone else around them, let alone make new friends. Parents who had been in the NICU long enough were so deep in their own experiences that a new arrival like me, filled with fear, was more than they could take. Plus, the physical setup of the ward didn't help. It allowed privacy with your baby but didn't present many opportunities to meet other parents.

At Alta Bates, the family room was the only place where a parent might get to know someone else. Usually parents were in the family room to get a quick bite of food or to take a moment away from the sounds of the NICU room. For me, it was a place to sit with some quiet. When I was there, the last thing I wanted to do was talk to other people. There were days, however, when I craved the chance to talk to someone else who might understand what I was going through. I was lucky enough that on just such a day, the other person in the room was also having one of those days when she wanted to talk.

That is when I met my NICU buddy, Elisa.

I had only been a NICU parent for less than two weeks. Elisa and I sat across the table from each other, sizing one another up. She looked remarkably put together. When she walked in, her black maxi dress just kissed the floor. Her long hair looked like she had just come back from the salon. Her eyes were tired but kind.

"Hi."

"Hi."

"How old is your baby?" I asked.

That was the easiest way to figure out if the person you were meeting was going to be a potential NICU friend. The last thing I wanted was to make friends with someone who was only going to be there for a short time.

"Thirty-one weeks. Yours?"

"Twenty-four weeks."

And with that, Elisa's face changed from one of a total stranger to a person filled with compassion and understanding. We talked for about thirty minutes, and in that time, I learned the basics of her story and the fact that she too had a little girl in kindergarten.

It was an immediate bond. She came over to meet Sam, and later that day I stopped by the isolette to meet her boy, Bennett.

For the rest of our overlapping time in the NICU, we would stop by each other's rooms to check in on each other and our boys. During long hours sitting next to our sons' isolettes, Elisa and I texted status updates to each other. I knew how many liters of oxygen Bennett was on and his oxygen saturation rate. Elisa knew how many bradys and apneas Sam had. We shared preemie clothing, herbs to keep our milk production up, and, eventually, when Elisa's milk supply finally called it quits, I gave her some of my overflow milk to help keep Bennett on breast milk till he made it to his six-month birthday.

Elisa and I became "war" buddies—surviving in the trenches of the NICU together. To this day, the boys see each other often—and when either of our kids has a medical issue, our first call is to each other.

Having someone who got it, and was not my husband, was everything. I can't imagine what the NICU and life after the NICU would have been like if we hadn't found each other.

Chapter 23

Irene seemed to be coping with our new reality better than I was. Here she was, taking care of me, making presents for Sam, and living her life. I, on the other hand, was doing my best to hold it together, but what I needed was a good long ugly cry. For some reason, I had convinced myself the only way to get through everything was to hold in my emotions. I think I was terrified that if I let them out, they would overwhelm me and I would not be able to function.

So, after a three-week break, I got my dad to drive me to my therapy appointment. I walked in, took one look at the therapist who had been with me since I lost the twins, and burst into tears.

I am not sure I said much more to her than "hi" and "bye." It was hard to speak as I was bawling like a baby. But that hour-long cry fest did more to help me feel better than anything up to that point. I released so much of the pent-up fear and was able to walk away having not vanished into an emotional abyss.

It was a good thing I got my cry session in when I did. By the time my dad got me to the hospital, things with Sam were looking a little grim. After eight short days of life, Sam was exhausted. His bradys were going up, and the doctors were worried that breathing on his own was taking too much out of him. The respiratory therapists and the neonatologist were discussing whether or not to put Sam back on the ventilator for the weekend. Just as adults get a break from their jobs, the idea was to give Sam a break from the chore of remembering to breathe.

Since I was there, and because holding Sam when he was on the ventilator was not the easiest, I settled in for a snuggle. The moment a nurse placed him on my chest, his numbers started to improve. His heart rate and oxygen saturation levels normalized, and his breathing evened out.

We stayed like that for over an hour. In that time, Sam not only didn't have a single brady, but his oxygen levels never dipped below ninety-eight. When we put him back in his isolette, he continued the stable numbers trend. This was encouraging to the doctors, so they agreed to watch and wait before putting him back on the ventilator. I made everyone I could find promise me that they would call me before re-intubating Sam.

With their assurances, I headed home for some quality time with my electronic baby.

Pumping had become an odd ritual for me. Normally with a newborn, you don't really think about your supply. Your whole life is baby cries, baby eats, baby stops crying, baby's had enough food. But when you are pumping, you are hyperaware of how much milk you produce. In my case, the total volume per day was fine. It was the volume per pump that had me cracking up.

I had schizophrenic boobs.

One pumping session, I would get a total of 225 milliliters, the next 20 milliliters, the one after that 154 milliliters, then just 14 milliliters. While I was hitting the recommended output of between 700 to 900 milliliters a day, I was doing it in a most erratic way.

Sam held strong the rest of that day, and the ventilator threat remained just that: a threat. By morning, he was exceeding all expectations and continuing on the medically stable path. He'd had only a handful of bradys overnight, and all of them were self-correcting. The doctors assured me that if Sam kept up this trend, they would not put him back on the ventilator.

It was clear to me that Sam's stubborn streak had kicked in. Anyone who knows me knows I don't like being told I can't do something. I find it inspiring to not only get the thing done but to do it well. I think Sam—every bit my son—heard he couldn't handle being off the ventilator and thought to himself, *Oh, hell no!*

Since Sam was doing so well, Peter, Irene, and I pretended our lives had not just been turned upside down and went out to breakfast as we normally did every Saturday. It was nice to be together as a family, eating pancakes.

After breakfast, we all went to Irene's soccer game before going back to visit Sam.

It sounded like the perfect break I needed. When we arrived, however, a few of the parents approached me to see how things were going, and I was immediately emotional.

As my tears started to well up, one of the moms swooped in, ushered everyone away, then gave me a wink and a smile. She had seen me break down at back-to-school night and knew that even the most well-meaning people could overwhelm me. With my guardian angel protecting me, I sat down on a bench, basked in the warm September sun, and enjoyed the normalcy of watching my kid play soccer.

Irene smiled as she trotted around the field and ran over to check on me every few minutes. At the end of the game, she sat next to me on the bench and wrapped her arms around me.

"I love you, Mommy," she said as she nuzzled her head into my chest.

"You are my angel, kiddo," I told her, squeezing her just a little tighter.

We both left the park with big smiles on our faces, refreshed and ready to face whatever the day was going to throw at us.

We took Irene to my parents' house for a grandparent playdate that afternoon, allowing both Peter and me to go to the hospital to see Sam. When we got there, Sam was still looking really good, having only had two bradys all day. Since he was stable, I wanted to get my cuddle in but knew I was going to have to pump before that. I went to the pumping room, did my thing, and trotted down to the freezer to "deposit" my milk.

When I opened the freezer door, I saw that I had filled all three milk storage bins the hospital had allotted me. A staff member approached me.

"Ah. So you are Harris," she said.

"Yes. Is there another bin I can have?" I asked.

"I have been meaning to talk to you. You are over your limit here. From now on, you will need to store your milk at home. We will let you know when you can bring more in."

"Guess I better clear out our freezer, because the milk factory is moving in!" I smiled.

I saw Misty walking by and called out, "Is it common for a mom to be banned from bringing in milk after just nine days?"

"No," she answered resoundingly.

Beaming with joy, I realized all my fears over my milk supply were unfounded. At least the doctors were upping Sam's feeds every day and I could hope he would consume all my milk. Sam was now taking four milliliters, almost a full teaspoon, every three hours.

Peter and I went back to Sam's room for a mommy cuddle. We

arrived just in time for his diaper change. On weekends, Sam's main nurse was Gay. She reminded me of the helpful school librarian. Knowledgeable, kind, supportive, stern when appropriate, and always ready with a hug of support.

"His balls dropped!" Gay announced joyfully when we walked in.

"Excuse me?" Peter choked out.

"I was changing his diaper and noticed that his balls had dropped. That's wonderful," Gay responded.

Now, among the things I never thought I needed to think about, balls dropping were high on the list. Apparently in preemies, balls dropping are a big deal, as sometimes surgery is needed to accomplish this task. Luckily for us, Sam took care of this act on his own.

With Sam in a fresh diaper, I got ready for our cuddle. I settled into the rocker and looked at Gay expectantly. She gave me this look and said, "It's time for you to do it yourself."

"Are you serious?" I asked, terrified that she would say yes.

"Well, you are his mom. Act like it," she said with a smile.

"So, I just, pick him up. Me. Just like that?"

"Yep. Be careful of all the wires, but otherwise, yep. Just like that."

So, for the first time, I got my son out of his isolette and placed him on my chest. It felt empowering to take him out, almost like I was his mom! We had a great cuddle (despite the postpartum-related sweat pouring down me). While he was snuggled up, Sam opened his left eye just a little. It was the first time I had seen his eye open, which made him look more baby-like.

I just watched him looking around, taking in the big world around him.

After one and a half hours of snuggling, I was finally ready to put Sam back.

"Gay, I am ready for Sam to go back," I said.

"OK. Why are you telling me?" she asked with a sly smile.

"You mean, I get to put him back in?" I asked.

"He is your baby. The more you do for him, the better."

Getting up while holding Sam was harder than sitting down with him. Peter had to support me under my arms to help me get to the standing position. Once up, I made the small walk from the glider rocker to the isolette and placed Sam back. It was an empowering feeling to have that much responsibility for Sam.

It was also time for a diaper change.

"I think Sam needs a new diaper," I told Gay once he was safely settled in his isolette.

"Again, why are you telling me? You know where the supplies are. Why don't you change him?" she responded.

While I was thinking, Peter jumped in and said yes. He got a quick lesson from Gay on how to change a preemie's diaper (pretty much the same as a full-term baby's diaper change, just on a smaller scale) and changed his son's diaper. I wish I had gotten a picture of the look on his face. He had a grin that only a proud papa taking care of his child for the first time can have—one part terror and one part joy.

We left the NICU that day on a high.

Chapter 24

Two days after the threat of Sam being put back on the ventilator, he was still doing great on the SiPAP. Sam spent the night on just 21 percent oxygen, which is basically room air. He also had a smaller number of bradys. There was one pretty severe cluster mid-morning, but his nurse extraordinaire, Gay, figured out that the bradys were caused by a feeding tube not sitting in the right place. After she corrected the tube placement, Sam had just one brady in four hours.

Despite Sam's stability, Gay was slightly concerned as she had noticed on a routine assessment that Sam had developed a heart murmur. She hadn't noticed it the previous day, and in his ten days of life, nobody had heard a murmur. Gay told us that the murmur was most likely caused by an open patent ductus arteriosus (PDA), a common issue in babies born between twenty-three and twenty-five weeks. Basically, a blood vessel near the heart opens when a baby is in utero to allow more blood to flow to the placenta. In a full-term baby, this blood vessel will close either at birth or within the first few days after birth. With preemies, this vessel often doesn't close on its own. Sometimes medication can cause it to close, but other times the baby will need surgery. The danger with an open PDA occurs when too much blood passes through the lungs, which can cause bradys or lung damage, puts a strain on the heart, and can reduce the amount of blood flow to the rest of the body.

Up until now, everyone had assumed that Sam's PDA was closed. That all changed with the appearance of the murmur. I tried not to let dread overtake my resolve to focus on the positives, but it was hard. Sam was so small, and the idea of surgery was terrifying. But, as I was learning, I had to take every minute in the NICU one at a time. Things changed quickly and there were no guarantees. For now, we would have to wait for an echocardiogram to see if his PDA was in fact open and how bad it was before deciding on the next course of treatment. The hope was to get the echo that day.

"I know it's hard to believe, but an open PDA is not as bad as it sounds," Gay said reassuringly. "In fact, it might be good news."

"How is that good news?" I asked, still trying to fight the terror rising in my chest.

"An open PDA could explain why Sam was having so many bradys. Once the PDA is closed, it's possible the bradys would stop."

"OK. That is something I can focus on," I said, feeling a bit more of the positive thoughts flowing.

With this news in hand, I took a little break in the lobby and ran into my Labor & Delivery nurse, Beth. This was the first time I had seen her since they'd wheeled me into the OR.

"Melissa!" Beth called out.

I started crying the minute I heard her voice. We hugged. This was the first time we had been able to hug.

"I have not been able to get any information on you since you went to the OR."

"Then you have to come up to the NICU and meet Sam!" I told her.

"I'll be there at my next break. I am so relieved to see you and to know that your baby is still here."

When I came back to the NICU, I let the staff know that Beth was allowed to visit Sam. After all she had done to care for me while I was hanging upside down in Labor & Delivery, I just knew this was a woman that our little man needed to meet.

That business taken care of, I headed to Sam's room for a little cuddle time.

When I walked in, Sam's growth chart caught my eye. When Sam was born, he was one pound, twelve ounces. In his first four days of life, he'd lost almost ten ounces, dropping him down to one pound, two ounces. Dr. Sandhu and Teresa constantly reassured me that losing weight in the first few days, while terrifying, was totally normal. Now, at ten days old, Sam was almost back to his birth weight at one pound, eleven ounces. I had to look at the chart twice to make sure I was reading it correctly. Convinced I had read it right, I called my mom to brag about Sam's weight gain.

At the end of my visit, my mom picked me up and took me home to help me pack a bag for Irene and myself. Peter had been called away on business, and with me still on a driving ban, I needed help taking care of Irene. I have to admit a big part of me was OK with having to go to my parents' house. Having my mom and dad around 24-7 to help take care of me sounded good. Besides, my parents were such a great help with Irene, and she loved spending time with them. If Irene could have had her way, we would all live under one roof so she could see her yayo and tutu every day.

Going to my parents' house was perfectly timed because my next day at the hospital was rough.

Things started off with Sam's echocardiogram. I arrived just as the tech was setting up. It's a painless test, similar to an ultrasound. That part went fine.

Once the echo was over, however, I settled in for my afternoon cuddle—and that was when things went downhill. While we were cuddling, Sam's oxygen level dropped and alarms started blaring. All of the color drained from Sam's body.

I panicked and froze.

Nurse Laura leapt into action, vigorously rubbing Sam's back while he lay limp on my chest.

After what seemed like an eternity, Sam's levels started to rise and his color returned.

"He's OK. He's breathing. You need to breathe too," Laura said with a reassuring hand on my shoulder.

Despite her best efforts, the damage to my calm was done. I was shaking and crying, and I just wanted to get the hell out of there.

"Do you want me to put him back?" Laura asked gently.

Unable to speak, I nodded. I was relieved when she lifted his tiny body off mine. I buried my head in my hands and wept. Laura didn't say anything, but she just stood there, with an arm on my shoulder, patting me. For that fleeting moment, the enormity of Sam's frailty was slapping me in the face.

Finally, I composed myself enough to stand up. I told Laura I was going to take a walk. I figured some fresh air would do me good. Unfortunately, as I was about to leave, Teresa came in and told me that the cardiologist had called with the results of the echocardiogram.

"Well, the news isn't great. Sam has a significant opening in his blood vessel that would require intervention," Teresa said.

My heart skipped. My palms began to sweat, and I started trembling again.

"The first step is to give Sam a course of Indocin to see if medication can close his PDA," Teresa continued. "We will give Sam three doses of Indocin over three days. On the fourth day, we will repeat the echocardiogram and see if the PDA has closed."

"And if it hasn't?" I asked.

"Then Sam will need to have surgery."

At the word "surgery," I had to sit down.

Teresa said that she was going to hold off on starting the Indocin for one day, since Sam's lab work showed elevated numbers, indicating his kidneys were working overtime. Indocin has a tendency to adversely affect kidney function, so she didn't want to start Sam on the medication until his kidneys appeared to be working normally. The elevated kidney numbers could be due to dehydration or to the open blood vessel.

The combination of a mini Bay Area September heat wave, exhaustion, and, well, being the mom of a micro-preemie had finally broken me. It was all too much. I just wanted to get out of there and crawl into the safety of my parents' home.

Overnight the doctors increased Sam's fluid intake to see if that would help his numbers. It didn't. At least Sam's A's and B's were better. As opposed to the previous night, Sam only had five bradys and his oxygen was set at 23 percent, only 2 percent above room air. Now, if Sam's blood work would just cooperate, Teresa would start the Indocin. By that evening, Sam's lab work was no better. They had to hold off for another day. I did not take this news gracefully. There was cursing, there were tears, and there was at least one thrown shoe. Luckily, I had this fit in the privacy of my parents' home.

Of course, the continued bad lab results were raising new concerns about Sam's kidneys. Teresa tried to reassure me that nothing she was seeing was out of the ordinary for a micro-preemie. To be safe, she ordered a kidney ultrasound for the morning. Now we had to make it through yet another night without starting the Indocin.

I would love to say I was the picture of grace and patience. All this waiting for his kidneys to get better so the doctors could fix his heart was frustrating. It was crazy to me that his kidneys could take precedence over his heart. I started ranking his organs in order of importance, and in my world, his heart trumped just about everything else. Despite my logic, Teresa, Laura, and Dr. Sandhu assured me that holding off on the Indocin was the way to go.

Finally convinced that all these doctors and nurses knew what they were doing, I decided the best thing I could do for Sam was to snuggle him close and bond with him, especially considering the disaster with the previous cuddle. Luckily, Sam cooperated, and we had a nice hour-and-a-half bonding session.

Those cuddle sessions had become so important for my well-being. Getting Sam's tiny little body next to mine helped to melt away my fear, anxiety, and stress. Just one short cuddle replaced everything bad with hope and love.

Unless of course Sam didn't cooperate. Too many A's or B's and the cuddle would send me into a tailspin.

When Peter and I were first introduced to life in the NICU, Misty made sure we understood that it would be a constant dance of "one step forward, two steps back." Dr. Sandhu told me that being a parent to a preemie is like constantly riding a roller coaster, climbing up, up, up with positive news and then plummeting all the way back down with bad news.

Our first week in the NICU was so easy and smooth; it was hard for me to see what they were talking about. Then the PDA issue presented itself, and everything changed.

On Day 13, I walked in and was startled to find Sam in the middle of his second blood transfusion. His first transfusion was on his second day of life. That one didn't bother me. This one got to me. I think part of it was how unexpected it was. No one had warned me that Sam might need another transfusion. The other part was seeing how much the transfusion seemed to agitate Sam.

Standing next to his isolette, watching Sam arch his back and flail his arms was enough to cause bile to rise in my throat and tears to flow from my eyes. Laura and Teresa were great with me, helping me pull it together as best I could. They explained to me that the amount and the pressure of the blood flowing through his body was just not what it should be, and that was causing a number of issues. The effects of the PDA finally started to present themselves in a reduced platelet count and an increase in the number of times Sam's heart rate and oxygenation levels dropped too low.

Despite my tears, I stayed with Sam all day, talking to him and just trying to keep him calm. With each minute, his agitation diminished and his numbers started to improve.

Well, most of his numbers. His kidney function was still out of whack. The ultrasound also showed a little issue with one kidney, but Dr. Sandhu and Teresa felt that was tied to the PDA, so they were not concerned.

It was then that I realized how glad I was not to be the doctor. Sam's PDA could be causing the kidney issues, which were preventing him from getting the Indocin, which could close the PDA, which could improve the kidney function. Wow.

Dr. Sandhu's plan was to check the kidney numbers in the morning as well as repeating the echocardiogram to see if the PDA had started to close on its own. From there, he would make the tough call on whether to start the Indocin or wait for Sam's kidneys to improve.

By the time I got home, between the worrying and the crying and the effort I was exerting not to worry and cry, I was exhausted. Luckily, my exhaustion had no impact on our family's ability to eat. Since I first entered the hospital, our community of friends and family ensured that the one thing neither Peter nor I had to worry about was food. Between groceries randomly showing up on our front porch and hot meals being delivered every other night, we were eating better than we normally did. On this particular night, I came home to find a delicious vegetarian chili, homemade cornbread, and a pile of blondies waiting, all courtesy of my friend Lisa. The warmth of that bowl of chili, and knowing that it was made especially for us, felt like a loving hug. I went to sleep recharged and ready for the coming day.

Now, if only the roller coaster of the NICU would take pity on me and give me a calm day. I closed my eyes and begged the universe to give me just one day without any excitement. I didn't need much, just a day with no crisis.

When I woke up, I gritted my teeth, crossed my fingers, and dialed the NICU.

"Good morning, Melissa," Laura chirped into the phone.

"You are in a good mood," I responded.

"Sam had an uneventful night, and has been totally boring all morning," Laura told me.

"I'll take that!"

"I'm not done," Laura interjected. "We just got his labs back, and his kidneys have shown enough improvement that Dr. Sandhu has ordered the Indocin."

"Way to bury the lede, Laura!"

I was hopeful that the Indocin would close that PDA right away, and Sam would start to improve. If that happened, then they could advance his feedings, and we could get him the hell out of there. While on the Indocin, Sam would be cut off of all breastmilk feeds and would have to rely on the supplemental nutrition. The idea was to reduce any stress on his body, like having to figure out how to digest breast milk. Poor guy.

Knowing that Sam was stable, I allowed myself the luxury of sitting around my quiet house for an hour and then had Lisa come over to share a cup of coffee and a chat. Plus, I wanted to thank her in person for the yummy meal she had brought the other day.

Sitting with Lisa in my living room felt decadent and was a much-needed mental recharge.

After a good two and a half hours of normalcy, she dropped me off at the hospital. I was ready to face whatever this new day was going to bring.

Walking into Sam's room, I was confronted with something I had not seen: Sam was looking around his room, alert, with both eyes wide open. Up until now, only one eye had been able to open. Seeing both eyes open was exactly what I needed to get my confidence back.

Sam was having a good day, and with both eyes open, he looked more like a normal baby, so I decided it was time for Irene to come back to the hospital and see her brother. Since Sam was born, Irene had only seen him that one time. We had not let her visit him since then, as we wanted to make sure Sam was in a better place so as not to scare Irene. With Peter at work, I called my parents and asked them if they would be willing to get Irene from school early and bring her to the hospital.

They jumped at the chance. Not long after the school day ended, my dad and Irene came barreling into Sam's room. Irene came with a huge smile on her face and presents: the bead heart she had made and a fuzzy blanket.

Early on in Sam's NICU stay, the nurses gave me blankets and a scent doll, which is nothing more than a small blanket knotted off to create a "head" and a "body," which I promptly renamed the stink doll, to take home and sleep with. The idea was to cover these items with my scent. Each morning when I arrived in the

NICU, I would replace the stink doll and blanket in Sam's isolette with the one I had slept with the previous night. This allowed Sam to be surrounded by the comforting smells of his mommy when I was not there. Irene had decided a few nights before that it was just as important for Sam to know the scent of his big sister, so she had been sleeping with one of his blankets. Now she proudly presented it to her little brother, excited for him to get to know her.

We spent about an hour at the hospital together as a family. Even in the unnatural environment of the NICU, having both my kids together in one place felt so right. The smile on my face made my cheeks hurt, but it was so worth it. I got the chance to be a mom to both of my children, at the same time, in the same room.

With a great family visit under our belt and Sam responding well to the Indocin, it finally started to feel like the NICU roller coaster was on its way up.

When I called the next day, once again Laura was happy to report that Sam was responding well to the Indocin, his kidney functions continued to improve, and the chest X-ray Teresa had ordered was the best yet. His lungs looked clear and healthy, an indication that his heart function was already improving. And, just to pile on the happy news, Sam was back on 23 percent oxygen after being in the 30s the past few days.

Laura told me Sam was stable enough, so I should come in and get my snuggle fix.

This time, Stephanie was my ride, which was great, as it meant she was finally going to get to meet Sam. Hard to believe it took fifteen days to introduce these two. She was there when he was born, but she'd never had a chance to meet him. After that, the combination of her busy life and her fear had kept her away. I sometimes forgot how abnormal all of this was for people—and how scary it was to see this little baby hooked up to all these machines.

I first introduced Stephanie to Sonia and Allison at the front desk.

"This is Sam's auntie," I told them proudly.

"Welcome, Auntie," they both said in unison.

I showed Stephanie the NICU way of washing hands.

"Now I see why your nails got destroyed. You have to do this every time you leave the NICU?" she asked.

"Not just leaving the NICU. I have to do this every time I leave Sam's room."

"Jesus."

From there we walked around the corner to where Sam's room was. I introduced Stephanie to Misty and Teresa. They already knew all about her, so they were happy to put a face to the stories. We then slid the glass door open to Room 11.

"Laura, this is the Stephanie I have told you all about. Steph, this is the amazing Nurse Laura." I felt like I was introducing two celebrities. At this point, Laura and Steph were two of the most important women in my life.

After a quick exchange of pleasantries, I asked Steph if she was ready. With a little smile, I pulled back the quilt that was covering the isolette, revealing Sam.

Steph took a small step back.

"You OK?" I asked.

"Seeing the pictures is one thing. He is just so . . . so . . . small," she answered.

"Be glad you were not here a few days ago," I said, trying to bring a little levity to the room.

Steph moved in for a closer look.

"He has the cutest little fingers." Steph smiled.

Just then an alarm went off. Both Laura and I glanced at the monitor and quickly went back to what we were doing. It was just a minor desaturation that was already self-correcting. Stephanie didn't look as calm.

"Yeah. That happens a lot. You get used to it," I explained, trying to reassure her.

"I don't know how you do this every day," she said, and pulled me in for a big hug.

When Stephanie dropped me off at home, I walked into what felt like a war zone. Peter and Irene were each on different sides of the living room. Peter sat on the couch, his arms folded, his face flushed. Irene was sitting on the floor, staring at nothing, her eyes red and swollen. Neither was speaking, but their body language said volumes.

"Hi. Is everyone OK?" I gently asked.

Peter threw his hands up in the air and said, "Ask your daughter!"

So I did.

At first, all I could get from her were surly one-word responses. Those soon degraded into tears and wails. Finally, I got Irene calmed down enough so I could understand what she was trying to tell me.

"Mommy, please don't make me go back," she wept.

"Go back to school?" I asked.

"NO! I don't want to go back!" Her body tightened as she fell onto my lap.

"Sweetie, are you talking about the hospital?"

"Yes . . . I never want to go back there!"

"Why, baby?"

"It's scary and I don't like it."

And with that, my big, strong almost-six-year-old collapsed into my lap, sobbing. We stayed like that until she was calm again.

I took her head in my hands, looked her in the eyes, and said, "You don't ever have to go back if you don't want to."

Immediately Irene's body relaxed, and she raised her head up to meet my gaze and asked, "Are you mad at me?"

"God no. I am so proud of you. I am sorry for not thinking about how scary Sam must seem to you."

You could immediately see the relief wash over her face. Irene had been trying so hard to be what she thought we wanted her to be. Finally being able to tell us how she felt had freed her from it.

While our conversation broke my heart, I was so proud of Irene for trying to put on a brave face for all of us and for finally telling us the truth. Hopefully now, with her fears out in the open, she would be honest with us, and herself, about how she was feeling.

Chapter 25

Day 16 in the NICU ended with a phone call from Laura. Thanks to caller ID, my heart would jump into my throat every time I saw "Alta Bates Summit" on the display.

This time, however, the news wasn't about Sam's health—thank God. Instead, Laura was informing us that Sam was going to move rooms that evening. In our first few days in the NICU, we had been told that babies get shuffled around the NICU all the time. In fact, it was rare to be in the same room for as long as we had been in Room 11.

A larger room with a window had opened up in a different part of the NICU, and the person in charge of room assignments thought we would like the new space better. For some reason, this news unsettled me. Room 11 had been good to us. Why mess with it? Like my dad had always told me growing up, never talk about a no-hitter when you are in the middle of seeing one pitched. You just don't want to mess with the juju.

When I called to check on Sam right before bedtime, his nurse, whom I had never met, told me Sam had had quite a few apnea events over the last few hours. That was enough for me. I began to pace back and forth in front of our bed, rambling about how the room switch had messed with the NICU juju, which was now putting Sam in danger of something bad happening to him.

From there, I got really irrational.

"Do you want me to go to the hospital to check on him?" Peter offered.

All that did was piss me off. I wanted to go check on Sam, but I couldn't because I was still not allowed to drive, which meant the only way to get there was a ride. It was late at night, and one of us had to stay home with Irene, who was soundly sleeping. I had no way of getting there.

If I was irrational before, now I was totally off the rails.

"Really? That is your response to me wanting to see Sam—you going?" I screamed at Peter. "What kind of..."

Peter left the room before I could finish my statement. I sat there in shock. He'd just walked out on me. I knew I was being a bitch, but I could not believe he would just walk out on me. Just as I was about to go find him, he came back to our room.

"Get dressed."

"Why?"

"I called Jeannie, and she is going to take you to the hospital."

I was shocked. Peter had walked away, called our next-door neighbors, and asked them to help get me (and my hysteria) to the hospital. Jeannie had jumped at the chance to not only help us but also to meet Sam.

I could barely muster a thank-you. I sniffled out something inaudible and hugged him.

I walked into the NICU, convinced I would find Sam in distress. Instead, I found him perfectly stable and learned that he had been fine since I called. My heart rate started to normalize, and I was able to finally take nice, even breaths. Despite my concerns about the room change, Sam was okay, and I had to admit the new room was nice and big, with a great view of the University of California campus and the iconic Campanile.

My zen didn't last long as I realized Sam was now in a part of the NICU staffed by an entirely different set of nurses. This meant all the nurses I had learned to trust, including Laura, would no longer be assigned to his case.

This really upset and confused me. When we first began our time in the NICU, Misty had told us to find nurses we liked and trusted and designate them as primaries. By now we had built up a pretty long list of primary nurses and had seen the value in the continuity of care. Having Sam in a different part of the NICU with all new nurses was just unacceptable.

But it was late, and I had already been on the emotional ledge, so I let it go—until the next day.

When Peter and I arrived at the NICU the following afternoon, we were greeted by two unfamiliar faces. It was a weekend, and we expected to see Gay taking care of Sam. Instead, we had two new nurses to deal with. I put my guard up. When I went to look at Sam's chart, I noticed a high number of apnea events.

"Are there any theories as to why there was such a marked increase in apnea events?" I asked the new nurse.

"It's probably because you tired Sam out the previous day doing kangaroo care," she responded.

Not a good first impression—blame the mom!

"Excuse me? I only held him for thirty minutes," I said defensively. "He normally will be on my chest for over an hour."

"Well, I don't know him, so I am not sure," was her only response.

That was it for me. The rage I was feeling began to boil up, heating my face and making my palms sweat. I looked at Peter, gritted my teeth, and took off in search of the head nurse.

By the time I got to her, I had managed to push down the rage enough to speak calmly. I explained our displeasure with the move and our distaste and discomfort with the new nurses. To her credit, she figured out how to move Sam back to where we had been for the previous fifteen days. She assured me Sam would be moved back by the morning and things would go back to normal—or as normal as they can be in the NICU.

As for Sam's health, aside from the uptick in apnea events, he was holding his own. He'd had his last dose of Indocin, which meant he could start getting milk again. Dr. Sandhu would order a new echocardiogram in two days so we could see if the Indocin had any impact on his PDA. So far, it seemed as if the heart murmur was a little better, which was an indication that the PDA might be smaller. The number of bradys had also stabilized, with Sam having only four in the past fifteen hours.

When I returned on Monday, Sam was back in Room 11 with nurses I recognized. His numbers were stable, and his oxygen level was set to 21 percent—otherwise known as room air.

"I see you worked your magic and got my man back over here." Laura laughed.

"Damn straight. I am not doing this without you. I need you more than Sam does," I responded.

"Well, it seems to have worked. Sam's had only two mild bradys since moving back here last night. And, when the night nurse handed me her notes, she pointed out that she was not able to hear Sam's heart murmur. Neither was I."

"Holy shit. Really?" I asked. "You mean the Indocin might have worked?"

"So far, it looks like it may have." Laura smiled.

"Holy shit."

"And . . . Sam has grown so much since he got here that he is now too big for the extra-small preemie diaper. We had to move him up to the small preemie diaper," Laura said proudly.

That meant that he was no longer in a diaper the size of my palm but was in a diaper the size of a checkbook. And, since he'd had the last dose of Indocin, Teresa wrote the order to start him back on two milliliters of milk every two hours.

With all this good news under my belt, I sat in the glider rocker next to Sam's isolette and hooked myself up to the electronic baby. I had timed things perfectly, so when I was done pumping, the milk would be given to Sam right away. The lucky little guy was going to get the freshest milk possible for his first meal in four days.

My plan was to snuggle with Sam as soon as I had finished cleaning up my pumping supplies.

Me and my plans.

As soon as I stood up and walked to the sink to clean up the supplies, the shit hit the fan. Just like when I miscarried the twins, I felt a huge gush of blood and clots passing.

Since my C-section seventeen days ago, I had been having mild bleeding, but this volume was startling. When I made it to the bathroom, I found four tennis ball–sized blood clots had passed. I sat there in the bathroom for a few minutes, looking around wildly, trying to figure out what my next move was going to be. Finally, after the third person tried the door to the only bathroom in the NICU, I cleaned myself up and went looking for advice.

I was in a hospital surrounded by doctors and nurses, but the person I went to find was my NICU buddy, Elisa. I wandered into her son Bennett's room, and Elisa knew immediately that something was wrong. It turns out when you lose a lot of blood, it shows on your face and in your skin color. I was ashen and had a wild, panicked look on my face. I told her what happened, and Elisa did what any rational person would do: she grabbed the nearest nurse. That nurse told me to go down to Labor & Delivery and get checked out.

I walked slowly through the halls of the NICU and out to the elevator. My legs were a little shaky, and I was worried I would have another huge loss of blood in the middle of the hallway. Besides, my mind was racing between flashbacks to my miscarriage and the bleeding that had brought me to the hospital before delivering Sam.

When I arrived at Labor & Delivery, the person at the desk gave me this funny look when I told her I was sent down by the NICU.

"How far along are you?" she asked, obviously not making the I-was-sent-from-the-NICU connection.

"No. I am not pregnant. I have a baby in the NICU who was born seventeen days ago. I am experiencing major bleeding and was told to come here."

"Yeah. We can't help you here. You need to go to the ER. Just make sure to tell them that you are experiencing severe post-op bleeding."

Great. The ER was down two more floors and on the other side of the hospital. I took a deep breath and began the trek. I would have given anything for an orderly and a wheelchair. I was so tired, and my throat was tightening up with fear, flashbacks, and anxiety. As I got closer to the ER, I reached for my phone to let my parents and Peter know what was going on.

I then walked myself into the ER.

"Can I help you?" the front desk person asked.

Remembering what the nurse in Labor & Delivery told me, I explained, "I am experiencing severe post-op bleeding."

"When was surgery?"

"Seventeen days ago," I responded, leaning more on the desk than before.

The person at the front desk could see me leaning and went to get a wheelchair for me to sit in. Once I was in the chair, they took me straight back into triage. One check of my blood pressure and I was moved immediately to a room.

The moment we got to the door to the room, I started to shake, my mouth ran dry, and I found myself struggling to breathe. This was not just any ER room. No. This was the same damn ER room where I had miscarried the second twin. I was too dumbfounded to tell the nurse and to beg her to take me to another room.

So here I was, with a micro-preemie in the NICU, bleeding profusely, worried, tired, and alone in the same fucking ER room where I had miscarried my twins. By the time Peter made it to the hospital, I was near catatonic. Between all the crying and blood loss, I had nothing left in me. I was lying on my side in my hospital bed, staring at the walls, unable to even acknowledge Peter's arrival. After some time, I turned my head toward him and whispered that I needed to pee, but that I just couldn't bring myself to go into that bathroom. He hadn't made the connection yet.

"I am not going in that bathroom," I insisted.

"Why not? If you need to pee . . . pee."

He hadn't meant to sound cruel, but his words stung.

"I am not going in *that* bathroom," I said more forcefully.

"Melissa . . ."

I cut him off before he could finish.

"I will not go back into the bathroom where I lost the twins!" I shouted.

He finally understood. Who could blame me for not wanting to go back to the same toilet where I had lost the second twin?

Peter laid out my options. I could use a bedpan, or he could hold my hand and walk me to the bathroom. I hated the idea of a bedpan. I hated the idea of that bathroom. But I had to pee. I finally opted for the bathroom.

Peter gently took my hand, helped me off the bed, and then

guided me to the bathroom. He stood there with me, stroking my hair while I peed and cried.

Being back in that same bathroom triggered even more emotional upset than I was expecting. I was overcome with visions of the baby hanging out of me—and kept hearing in my head Peter screaming for a doctor. I trembled as I sobbed. Peter just stood there. He still had no idea what it was I saw the day I miscarried the twins—and I was not going to tell him. It was all too much, physically and emotionally.

When our ER nurse came in to check on us, she saw how agitated I was and asked Peter what was wrong.

"This room is the same room we were in when she miscarried our twins a year back."

"Oh God."

"Is there another room we can go to?"

"I can check—but we are pretty full right now."

Nurse Sunny (yes, that really was her name) left to see what could be done. She came back quickly and let us know that the only other option was a bed in a room with another patient. By this time, I was already so exhausted and overcome with all of the trauma of the room that I opted for the privacy—and a sedative—as opposed to a roommate.

Soon after the sedative took effect, my mom arrived. While a husband is good, at times like this, a mom is always better, especially one as supportive and caring as my mom. Peter quickly filled her in on the situation and why I had been sedated. Now that I was calm and drooling just a little, the nurse came to take me to ultrasound. The ultrasound technician was the same one who had done my first ultrasound the day I arrived in Labor & Delivery. We remembered her, and after a quick chat, she remembered us. As Peter and the tech talked, I drifted in and out. The sedative had made me tired, but my mind was still racing—reliving the miscarriage and all that had happened since then.

The ultrasound tech told us that she saw something she wanted her supervisor to see. Her supervisor confirmed something didn't look right.

Here we were in a familiar situation: an abnormal ultrasound and no real explanation.

I was wheeled back to my "favorite" room in the ER, where my mom was waiting.

A few minutes later, the ER doctor came in to let us know that they were going to admit me. I needed a D&C to remove the "products of conception" that were left in my uterus. This was what the tech had seen on my ultrasound. Apparently, a portion of the placenta was still inside me, which was causing the bleeding.

Not fifteen minutes after that, the ER doctor was back to tell me she had been overruled.

"So, the OB on call doesn't want you admitted."

"Why? If there is something wrong, shouldn't it be fixed?" my mom asked.

"Well, the OB on call says he knows your case. Do you know Dr. Wharton?" she asked.

"Yes, he is the one who did the C-section," Peter answered.

"Well, Dr. Wharton is confident that there is no way he left anything in your uterus and that you have been traumatized enough."

I appreciated his confidence.

"He is ordering a medication that will make your uterus contract and help push out whatever blood and clots might be remaining. He was not concerned at all about what he saw on the ultrasound. It is his opinion that it is nothing more than a big clot that has yet to pass."

So, six hours later, sedation still in effect, I came home to sleep it off.

The following morning, I was cramping up a storm, thanks to the medication, but it seemed to be working, as I passed a couple of really large clots. Each clot that passed put me right back in the hallway of my office where I'd lost the first of the twins or into the ER bathroom where I'd lost the second. Each cramp transported me back to the six days I laid in Labor & Delivery, trying to hold on to my pregnancy. There was a name for what I was experiencing; I just didn't know it yet: post-traumatic stress disorder (PTSD).

Despite my crampiness, there was no way I was not going to see Sam. I called and found out he had started to show some negative side effects from the Indocin. His kidney function was slowing down, so his urine output was very low. Dr. Sandhu and Teresa had warned us that the Indocin could negatively impact his kidneys.

Peter sat on the edge of our bed, his hands resting on the tops of his legs, and inhaled deeply. He was preparing himself to try and convince me I needed to rest, not take a trip to the NICU.

"You *were* in the ER yesterday, you know," he said.

"Your point being?"

"Don't you think you should rest and, I don't know, recover a little?"

"No. No, I don't. Now, do I need to call for a ride, or are you going to drive me?"

Peter put up a good fight, but I wanted to be there if Sam was starting a downward path. Sam needed me—and I needed to be with him.

Peter smiled weakly, as he knew how this debate was going to end, and headed to the garage with me close behind.

We spent three hours next to Sam's isolette, holding his little hand and talking to him. At one point, Elisa came over to check on Sam and was startled to see me there.

"Um, weren't you in the ER yesterday?"

"Yes . . . but I am fine. I swear." I was lying. I was tired and cramping and bleeding, but I was not going to tell anyone that.

"You look like shit. You need to go home and rest," Elisa said bluntly.

"I second that," Teresa chimed in from the room next door.

"I third it," Misty added.

"You don't even want to get me started, do you?" Laura said, looking me square in the eye.

"I take it you all think I should go home and rest?" I said, resigned to my fate.

And just like that, Peter swooped in and said it was time to go. Apparently, he had been too scared to make me leave, but with Elisa, Misty, Teresa, and Laura all ganging up on me, he knew I was outnumbered and would not argue.

Not long after we got home, the phone rang. It was Teresa. Sam's kidney function was starting to concern the doctors. They had drawn some blood and ordered an ultrasound.

Two hours later, the phone rang again. This time it was the overnight neonatologist. Sam's red blood cell count, or hematocrit, was really low, and the preliminary blood work showed signs of an infection. They were starting him on antibiotics and were going to give him a blood transfusion, his third since being born.

"Look, I know I need to rest, but I can't. Please, Peter. I have to go to the hospital." I was begging at this point.

"You are no good to Sam if you are not taking care of yourself."

"I am not able to take care of myself if Sam is declining. Don't you get that?"

"I'm scared too," Peter added, clearly hurt that I didn't think he understood.

"Sam needs us with him. He needs to hear our voices."

"OK. I know better than to argue with you. Let's call your parents."

My dad answered after the first ring.

"Sam isn't doing well, Dad," I cried.

"What do you need us to do?" he responded without hesitation.

"Can you come watch Irene so we can go to the hospital?"

"Only if you promise to send updates—often."

"Deal."

We got there right after the blood transfusion started, and we could see an immediate positive change in Sam. He perked up and moments later he peed for the first time in over a day, indicating that his kidney function was improving. All of this put us at ease, and after about an hour, I admitted I was totally exhausted and in dire need of about twenty-four hours of uninterrupted sleep.

Of course the electronic baby would only let me have three. Well, make that seven. I slept through two pumping alarms.

It took everything in me to finally get up the next morning. The NICU roller coaster was in full swing, and I felt dizzy and exhausted. Terrified about what I would hear from the NICU, I delayed making my daily "before getting out of bed" phone call. I figured if something really bad was going on, Laura would call me. Besides, I needed to pump and apologize for forgetting our wedding anniversary the previous day.

What can I say? The world of the NICU makes everything else just vanish. Thank God we have things like Facebook to remind us of all the things we otherwise would have forgotten. But the reality is it was more than just forgetting; our relationship was so strained from everything the past few years, I was in no mood to celebrate our marriage.

Peter laughed when I told him how sorry I was that I forgot our anniversary. He had forgotten too. We agreed to just postpone this year's anniversary.

With the anniversary issue settled and my pumping completed, I mustered up enough nerve and gave the NICU a call.

To my immense relief, all of the news was good. Sam had peed up a storm all night, meaning his kidneys were working again. The early results from the blood smear were positive for an infection, which could be the cause of the kidney issues.

The biggest news of the day was the decision by the respiratory therapist to move Sam from SiPAP to CPAP. Preemies usually go from the ventilator to SiPAP to CPAP to nose cannula to nothing. A CPAP delivers a continuous flow of air that aids in breathing, but the babies do most of the work themselves. SiPAP has two pressure settings that help regulate not just the oxygen intake but also the breaths per minute. Regardless of the difference, this was a big step forward for Sam.

Because Sam was in the NICU and no good news goes unpunished, Teresa called with one unsettling piece of news.

"Most of the news on Sam is good, but I am concerned that his infection may have migrated into his spinal fluid and become meningitis."

I took a deep breath.

"So what now?" I finally asked.

"Dr. Sandhu ordered a spinal tap so we can be sure."

It's hard to believe that there is a needle small enough to do a spinal tap on someone of Sam's size, but apparently there is. Unfortunately, getting the needle in the right place was not so easy.

"When will that be?" I asked.

"Well. We have already done it. Three times. The first sample was contaminated with Sam's blood."

"You have done this three times already?"

"Yes. Unfortunately, the next two were also contaminated. It's really hard when they are this small to get a clean sample."

"When will you try again?" I asked.

"Not going to. I don't want to put him through anything else today. To be careful, we have him on a broad-spectrum antibiotic. We may try again for a spinal tap in a day or two."

When I finally got to the hospital, Teresa told me they had also run a test on Sam's urine that came back positive for E. coli, one of the more common infections in preemies. Luckily, the broad-spectrum antibiotic he was on would also treat the E. coli. I decided to defer to them and join them in being happy that my son had E. coli. Yeah?

"He has had a tough day, but I think it would do him some good if you held him," Teresa said.

"I'll never say no to that." I smiled.

I gently took him out of the isolette and settled in for a lovely kangaroo cuddle. Having Sam's skin touching mine always brought me some peace of mind. For Sam, it usually brought a large number of farts, and in this instance, his first poop in almost twenty hours. Teresa was right. After I left, Sam had a totally mellow and uneventful day in the NICU.

The following day was more of the same: stable, mellow, and uneventful. Both Sam and I needed some calm days to rebuild our physical strength—and for me, my emotional strength. Those two days of calm became even more important, as the following day, Sam's twenty-first day in the hospital, is the one I will always remember as the day my rose-colored glasses were smashed to smithereens.

Chapter 26

When I arrived at the hospital, Sam's numbers were stable, and according to his nurse, he'd had only four bradys overnight, all of them self-correcting. Sam had been on CPAP for just two days, but he was responding so well, the respiratory team decided to take Sam off the CPAP and try him on a simple nose cannula. The nurses called this a "cannula sprint." My guess is they call it a sprint as it can be as exhausting for a baby as running the forty-yard dash can be for a sprinter.

Despite my unease at the idea of Sam doing all the breathing on his own with just a cannula, the respiratory team was confident that Sam was ready.

"We would not suggest this if we were not sure."

I nodded.

"To be extra sure, we have been waiting for you to arrive. We want to do the sprint while you are holding Sam. He is always at his most calm when he is on your chest."

The flattery worked wonders. I got settled into the glider rocker with Sam on my chest. I was terrified for Sam. This would be his first time without any form of forced air and breathing all on his own. It seemed like a lot to ask for a baby who didn't even weigh two pounds yet.

"We don't expect this to last long," the respiratory tech told me, "but it is really good for him and his lung development to try."

All of that fear melted away when the respiratory therapist took the CPAP mask off and slipped the cannula prongs into Sam's nose. Once again, I was treated to a view of my son's perfect and beautiful face. My God. He was beautiful. Yes, his nose was smushed after having a mask covering it for the past seventeen or so days. But the rest of his face was perfect. I sat there speechless, enjoying the "sprint."

Sam lasted about twenty-five minutes more than I thought he would. With the sprint done, Sam was put back onto CPAP. We would continue to do sprints as long as Sam was strong enough.

From the high of the cannula sprint, things started to go downhill. First, Sam had his fourth spinal tap in three days. Teresa made me leave the room for the spinal tap. I didn't mind. The idea of anyone putting a needle in Sam's spine was scary enough. No way I needed to watch it.

Luckily, this time they got a clean sample, and the preliminary results were mixed. It wasn't a clear yes that he had meningitis, but it wasn't a clear no either. They needed a full culture for a definitive answer, but in the meantime, Sam would stay on the broad-spectrum antibiotic for ten days, as well as start an anti-fungal medication. Being on broad-spectrum antibiotics makes babies susceptible to fungal infections, which can be really dangerous. If it's not one thing, it's another.

The biggest issue of the day, however, was Sam's kidneys. He had not peed since the night before, and once again the nurses, doctors, and Teresa were getting worried. Their concern had me concerned.

Then they took me from concerned to really scared.

Once a week, we had a team meeting with Teresa, Dr. Sandhu,

and Misty. This was protocol in the NICU, especially with one as small as Sam. Our meeting was set for midday.

"In many ways, Sam is doing very well," Dr. Sandhu started. "However, his kidney function is of grave concern."

"How grave?" Peter asked.

"Well, we need him to show improvement in his BUN and creatinine levels."

"Can you put this into terms we can understand?" Peter responded.

"His kidneys need to start working. If he doesn't pee in the next twenty-four to forty-eight hours, it could be fatal," Dr. Sandhu said as compassionately as possible.

Yes—he used the f-word. The word hit me hard, and it felt like all the air in my body left me at one time.

Up to this point, I'd known Sam was fragile and that the road was going to be rough, but it had never even occurred to me that death could be one of the possible outcomes for Sam.

With that reality now firmly facing me, I made up my mind not to leave the hospital until Sam peed. I didn't care how long that would take.

I needed to see him pee.

By 6 p.m., Sam still had not peed. At this point, I had been at the hospital for almost nine hours. Peter and my mom had traded places as my chaperone in the NICU. I was glad my mom was there because my facade of being cool and collected had crumbled around me, and I began to panic. The reality that Sam could die was staring me in the face. My heart raced, and a lump in my throat made it difficult to swallow. My eyes started to burn, and I could no longer hold the tears back.

My mom saw the tears streaming down my face and told me we had to get some air.

"You need to take a break," she said.

"I can't leave the NICU, Mom. I just can't."

"Well, you can't stay in his room. It's not good for you or Sam. Come on. A nurse set up two chairs for us right outside his door. Just for a few minutes."

I knew she was right. I knew I was about to begin sobbing, and I didn't want to do that in front of Sam. I needed to be strong in his presence. If I was a weeping mess next to his crib, who would he lean on for strength?

We sat down on the chairs, and my mom put an arm around me. I wept and lay my head on her shoulders. We sat like that, not speaking, for a while. I was so glad to have my mom there. For just that moment, I needed not to be an adult and a parent. I needed to be a child—taken care of by her mommy. Despite being in a bustling NICU, it was so quiet and still around us.

Then the door to Sam's room opened and the neonatologist on duty that night, Dr. Wu, came bounding out, jumping up and down, yelling, "He peed! He peed!" Dr. Wu is normally very quiet and reserved, so this scene really made an impression on me and everyone else who was in the NICU.

She wasn't sure whether the extra fluids or the antibiotic helped him. All she knew was that the little stinker peed.

Chapter 27

After the emotional roller coaster of the previous day, I was too scared to call the NICU the next morning. My nerves were frayed, and my emotions were ready to boil over. I was not sure I had it in me to go through another up and down day.

"Do you want me to take the day off and stay here?" Peter asked.

I didn't want to tell him that his presence didn't really help me.

"Only if you want," I replied. "Mom is planning on being with me today."

"Let's call and see what is going on with Sam. OK?" Peter asked.

"I am not quite ready to call. If it's bad news, I just . . . I just want a few more minutes not knowing."

I am not sure Peter fully understood, but he agreed to give me a few more minutes.

When I finally worked up the courage to call, Laura was on duty. She happily reported that Sam had peed and pooped for the night nurses and was looking pretty good today. With a HUGE sigh of relief, Peter headed to work and I called my mom to give her the update and confirm my ride to the hospital.

Mom and I got there around 11:30 a.m. Within about three minutes of our arrival, Sam had a terrible apnea event, where he couldn't breathe for what felt like several minutes. This one needed vigorous intervention from Laura.

It was the first of many he would have during the day. Perhaps the trauma of the previous day had tired him out and he needed to rest. Laura told me not to worry too much about the apnea events, but they were very hard to watch.

The plan for Sam was to bother him as little as possible all day. Laura would check his diaper regularly to look for pee and feed him a little breast milk through the feeding tube. There would be no kangaroo care, and the lights and noise in his room would be kept as low as possible. The only other activity was to get his second head ultrasound out of the way.

This plan seemed to work, as Sam put out an enormous amount of pee and had fewer and fewer apnea events. The best news of the day were the results of the head ultrasound: no brain bleeds at all. This was the second ultrasound to show nothing but a brain. The next ultrasound would not occur until Sam was about to go home, but for now, Teresa told my mom and me to breathe a sigh of relief.

I left the NICU encouraged and optimistic. It seemed like Sam had gotten through the worst, and all that was left was for him to grow and come home.

Oh, how foolish I was.

When I got up the next day and called the NICU, I learned that overnight Sam had begun to have problems holding his oxygen saturation levels. They upped his oxygen, but he still continued to have major apnea and brady episodes. While I was on the phone with one of the nurses in the room, Sam's oxygen level went down to just twenty-four (normal is one hundred), and despite vigorous stimulation, Laura had to manually breathe for Sam by "bagging" him. I could hear all of this commotion going on through the phone—until the nurse told me she would have to call me back when the situation was under control.

The five minutes it took for someone to call me back were awful. I was alone in the house, pacing around my bedroom, muttering to the cats that I didn't know if I would be able to hold on to my resolve much longer. Keeping my emotions suppressed was the only way I could get through every day. If the wall I had built up around my emotions cracked, and the floodgates opened, I feared I would drown and no longer be able to act as Irene and Sam's mom, let alone function.

Finally, with Sam breathing with the aid of the CPAP machine, Laura called me back.

"He's OK," Laura said in her most reassuring voice.

"It doesn't sound like it to me!" I squeaked out between my sobs.

"Melissa—I don't lie to you. He is OK. He is just tired."

"Still..."

"Listen, do you hear any alarms?"

I envisioned Laura holding the phone up to the monitors in Sam's room.

"No. I don't."

"See, he is OK. Now calm down and then come see for yourself."

Feeling a little better, I hung up the phone and called my dad to get a ride. I'd barely gotten my hello out when my dad asked me what was wrong, so I explained. Ever the pragmatist, my dad pointed out Sam was fighting an infection, had been doing cannula sprints, and oh yeah ... he was a micro-preemie.

"Get dressed. I'll come get you," Dad said once he felt I had calmed myself down.

When I got to the NICU, I left Dad at the sink, still working on his handwashing, and practically ran to Sam's room. Laura was waiting for me with a reassuring hug and a quick status update.

"Like I said, he is fine. No A's or B's since we talked."

"You guys scared the crap out of me," I replied.

"Well, your phone call was poorly timed," Laura said, smiling. "We are just going to let Sam be again today."

"I can work with that. I will just sit here with him, OK?"

"I expected nothing less," Laura answered.

I sat with Sam for four hours, just talking to him about the news of the day, what his sister was up to, anything really that popped into my head.

My dad sat watch over me, either in the room with us or at the doctors' table right outside the door to Sam's room. When my dad finally dragged me away, Sam was still stable, and I just had to have faith that he would stay that way overnight.

For the rest of the evening and into the next morning, I called the hospital every time I got up to pump and was pleased that Sam was holding his own. He was having a good night and responded well to being left alone. Even with that good report, Peter decided to take the day off of work so he could be with Sam and me at the hospital.

Not long after we arrived, Sam had another terrible apnea event. The scary thing is that without the monitors, you would never know something was wrong until it was really wrong. We were talking to Sam when all of a sudden his monitor started to beep. This was a normal part of being in the NICU, but the sound changes the worse the numbers get. By the time I looked at the monitor, Sam's oxygen levels were around thirty.

His nurse, Joanne, who was one of his afternoon primaries, stepped in and started to rub Sam's foot with her knuckles, trying to stimulate him. This didn't work. She then put her hand on his chest and tried stimulating him that way.

By now, the color was drained from Sam, and he looked ashen.

Joanne gave up on stimulating Sam and grabbed the bag to help him breathe. I had not seen this done before, so I knew something was different this time.

After a few squeezes of the bag, Joanne looked at us again and said, "I need you two to step out for a moment."

She said this in a very reassuring, sweet but firm way. As we walked out, all sorts of alarms went off, and nurses, doctors, and respiratory therapists came running to Sam's room. Despite Joanne's efforts, Sam was still not responding, and she'd had to push the crash button.

This was enough to set off my first ever panic attack. I stood outside of Sam's room, hyperventilating, doubled over, crying and emitting what can best be described as a guttural moan while I helplessly waited to hear that Sam was OK. I have no idea if Peter said anything to me or not; I was in a fog. I could feel his hand on my back, but that was it. Everything sounded far away. I knew people were talking, but their words were muffled.

Apparently, my wailing caught the attention of Alison, a clinical nurse specialist and nurse manager of the NICU. She and Peter gently guided me to a chair. I knew there were now two sets of hands on me, but I still could not make out any of the words they were saying.

After what felt like hours, Joanne came out of Sam's room.

"He is OK. He is breathing."

Those were the first words I could really make out. I looked up at her, trying to focus. She wrapped her arms around me.

"I'm so sorry for scaring you, Melissa. He was never in danger. I promise."

I cried harder.

"I needed additional support, and the crash button is the best way to get that support," Joanne continued.

I nodded.

"Come back and see for yourself. I promise. He is just fine."

Joanne gently ushered us back into Sam's room to see for ourselves. While Sam was breathing again, he looked terribly fragile.

"We should go home. You look exhausted," Peter said, breaking the silence.

I just nodded. I had nothing left in me.

Once in the car, Peter turned to me and said, "I want you to call your doctor. I think you might need a prescription for an anti-anxiety medication. You scared me back there."

I had not been in control of my body or my breathing. Peter wanted to make sure if this ever happened again, we were prepared for it.

The rest of the day, Sam continued to decline. His kidneys were not producing urine again, and his blood count was also down. The doctors started him on a medication to stimulate his kidneys and gave him a blood transfusion (his fourth) to help bring his blood count up.

It took everything in me to not go back to the hospital. My tank was on empty, and I needed to sleep. But I also felt the pull of the NICU. Not being allowed to drive was the only thing that kept me from going to the hospital, as Peter refused to take me back until I got some rest.

At 9 p.m., the phone rang. I knew it was the hospital before I even saw the caller ID.

"What's wrong?" I asked without saying hello.

A voice I didn't recognize responded, "Is this Melissa?"

"Yes. Is Sam OK?" I asked.

"He is OK, but his evening has been hard. There have been a number of apnea events, and we are going to give Sam a break and reintubate him."

There were no tears left to cry at this point.

"Thank you for letting us know. If anything changes, no matter the time, will you make sure someone calls?" I asked.

"Of course. Try and rest," she added before hanging up.

From the day Dr. Sandhu decided to take Sam off the ventilator when he was just three days old, we knew there was a chance he would have to go back on it. In theory, I understood that. The rest would be good for Sam. However, a piece of me viewed reintubation as a total defeat.

While the respiratory team was trying to reintubate Sam, they found a blockage in his throat, a severe mucus plug on top of his vocal cords that was blocking his airway and making it difficult for him to breathe. The moment the plug was out, Sam got a bit of his feistiness back and started to fight with the doctors.

Despite his improved state, the respiratory team reintubated him, just to give him a night off. The doctors were confident they would be able to remove the tube the next day.

Come morning, between the blood transfusion, the kidney medication, and the ventilator, Sam was stable and peeing, two good things.

We arrived at the hospital and were greeted by Dr. Sandhu.

"Hello, Melissa and Peter. Looks like Sam is doing much better today."

"Does that mean you will take him off the ventilator?" I asked.

"I don't think so. I think another day on the vent will give him some more time to improve."

It wasn't the answer I wanted to hear, but I think I understood.

"I need to tell you, when I last examined Sam, I detected the heart murmur again."

"So, the Indocin didn't work?" I asked.

"Let's see what the echocardiogram I just ordered shows. If the PDA has shown no improvement, we will need to schedule him for surgery."

I swallowed hard. "Does that mean he will need to be transferred to another hospital?" I asked. "I mean, how . . . Where . . . How . . ."

"The surgery is called a PDA ligation. It is very straightforward."

I scoffed a little. "Straightforward? Sam doesn't weigh two pounds."

"I know it's hard to imagine. But we have done this before."

"Tell me again how this works."

"A surgical team from Oakland Children's Hospital will come here to do the surgery. They bring with them an anesthesiologist, a pediatric cardiologist, a resident, and a specialized nurse. They will turn Sam's room into a sterile operating room. Sam will be given a paralytic and then sedated. The surgeon will create an incision behind his left shoulder to access his heart. The valve will be closed with a small clamp," Dr. Sandhu explained. "The entire procedure should take about thirty minutes."

It sounded easy for Sam, as he would be sedated, but terrifying for me, as I would not.

First thing the following morning, Sam had his echocardiogram. Dr. Sandhu called me with the results.

"Unfortunately, the Indocin has not done the trick. In fact, the PDA was more open than on the last scan. We can also see that Sam's heart is working too hard. If he doesn't have the surgery, he will not survive."

I knew this might be coming, but still, hearing it from Dr. Sandhu was terrifying. This was the second time he had mentioned that Sam might not survive, an outcome I refused to accept.

"I understand. I will be there as soon as I can. When do you think the surgery will be?"

"We have already arranged it. The surgery will be in two days,"

Dr. Sandhu informed me. "Melissa, I need you to understand that this will be a very hard week for Sam. He is likely to get worse before he gets better."

I spent the next day and a half pacing by Sam's bedside. I was excited to get this surgery done but worried at the same time. I understood surgery was the only way Sam was going to survive, but that didn't make it any easier. I was having a hard time believing that any doctor could operate on a baby that small without making some sort of mistake. One of the most common unintended outcomes of a PDA ligation was cutting the vocal cords. I was convinced this would happen to Sam and obsessed over it. It was easier to worry about Sam's vocal cords than to think about the fact that a doctor was going to be cutting into Sam's tiny little heart.

The night before the surgery, we took Irene to my parents' house for a sleepover. Peter and I needed to spend time at the hospital with Sam before the surgery, and we were going to need to be there early the next morning as well. Luckily, Irene viewed a sleepover at her grandparents' on a school night as a treat, not a punishment, so we got little argument from her.

With Irene happily tucked in at my parents', we headed for the hospital. It had been almost five days since I had been allowed to hold Sam, and I was really desperate to wrap my arms around him.

When we got there, he was looking really good, and his nurse told us that Teresa had written an order for me to hold Sam. Apparently, she felt it was as important for me to get my hands on Sam as I did.

Chapter 28

We arrived at the hospital by 6:30 a.m. Sam's room was bustling with nurses getting it ready to become an operating room. We were allowed in for a few minutes to say hi to Sam before we had to leave to allow the nurses time to finish sterilizing the room and setting up for surgery.

When we stepped out, a nurse greeted us with a tray of homemade chai. The tea was just what I needed, warm and inviting. Alison arrived soon after.

"The room across from Sam's is empty. We have put two glider rockers in there for you and Peter. You will be just across the hall," Alison told us.

We appreciated the gesture and welcomed the privacy. I was a nervous mess. Soon after we settled in, the surgeon arrived. He was exactly as Teresa had described: tall, bald, efficient, confident, and German.

"Hello, it looks like we are set to start. Do you understand what we will be doing?"

Peter and I both nodded.

"OK. Please sign the consent paperwork, and I will come back and see you when we are done. Don't worry. This is not my first PDA ligation." He smiled, trying to be reassuring.

Once the consent papers were signed, a nurse whisked us in to give Sam a kiss and just as quickly whisked us out. With that, we left our twenty-eight-day-old micro-preemie in the capable hands of the surgeon.

My parents had dropped Irene at school and had made their way to the NICU, settling in the family room. Mom came back to find us, and to let us know that my dad was happily working on the *New York Times* crossword puzzle in the family room. She also let us know that he had brought a carafe of coffee and pastries. It made me smile that no matter how worried Dad was, he had to have his morning coffee and crossword puzzle.

Even the lure of coffee and pastries in the family room couldn't get me to budge. I wanted to stay across the hall from Sam so I would be as close to him as possible. I figured while Sam was in surgery, I would pump and clean up before the surgeon was done.

It turned out the surgery took less time than it took me to pump. The surgeon knocked on the sliding glass door, poked his head in, and said, "It went great." That was it. Before we could even ask him a question, he was gone. I still had the pumping cones attached to my breasts.

As soon as he left, a nurse came in and told us we could come see Sam if we wanted.

Peter, who was not attached to an electronic baby, jumped at the chance, and left me alone to go check on Sam.

Not wanting to worry folks on the day of Sam's surgery, I had kept to myself the fact that I woke up with some slight cramping and had felt a little light-headed. By the time the surgery was over, I was starting to bleed a little and the cramps had gone from mild to severe.

As soon as I knew Sam was OK, I got up to clean the pumping supplies and take the milk to the freezer and then headed toward the family room to use the bathroom. Just as I got to the entrance of the family room and caught my father's eye, I felt a huge gush of blood and clots come out. Of course I was wearing light gray pants, so there was no hiding what was going on. My poor father, who was on the phone with my brother giving him an update, quickly hung up the phone and rushed to me.

I was ashen and covered in blood down to my knees.

He put his arm around me. "Where are we going?" he asked.

"I need to get to the bathroom," I replied weakly.

He helped me there and then grabbed the first NICU employee who walked by and told them we needed help . . . and a pair of pants!

I sat there on the toilet and felt clot after clot pass. The largest clot to come out was about the size of my hand. There were five or six smaller clots that also passed. It had been twelve days since my last bleeding episode and ER visit. This was worse. The bleeding was heavier and the clots were much bigger. I was terrified that I was going to have to be admitted and have a D&C. All I wanted was to put eyes on Sam and see for myself that he was OK. I just could not wrap my head around the fact that I was bleeding once again.

I can only imagine the chaos that was going on outside the bathroom door. A trail of blood needed to be cleaned up. My father tends to shut down when people he loves are in trouble, and now he had to worry about his daughter as well as his grandson. Peter was standing with my mom next to Sam's surgery bed when someone told him I was bleeding in the bathroom. They made a quick decision—Mom would come take care of me, and Peter would stay with Sam.

My mom arrived, followed quickly by Alison, who had found a pair of scrubs for me to put on.

"Melissa, I am paging your doctor. We are not letting you

leave here until we know what is going on," Alison told me, clearly in control of the situation.

"I need some towels. I am a mess, and the floor in here is a mess," I cried.

"Clean yourself—leave the floor."

"Honey, I need you to unlock the door so I can come in and help you," my mom said gently.

"I never even got it locked," I half laughed and half cried.

Mom came in and surveyed the scene. I, and the bathroom, were quite a sight. She helped me rinse out my blood-soaked pants, cleaned up my legs, got me into the scrub pants, and finally out the door.

Alison had a wheelchair waiting for me.

"We have set up one of the overnight rooms here for you. After you see Sam, you are to get in the bed and not leave it until you have been seen by a doctor."

My dad wheeled me down the hall to Sam's room. Peter grabbed me the moment he saw me.

"Don't you ever scare me like that again!" he cried as he knelt down next to the wheelchair, grabbed my shoulders, and sobbed. "I can't have both of you sick."

"I'm sorry."

"Don't be sorry, just don't do that again."

"I'll see what I can do," I said, trying to lighten the mood.

"I love you, goddamnit. You scared the shit out of me. Don't you get that?"

"Yes. I am sorry. I love you. I'm sorry," I cried.

Peter leaned in and gave me a kiss on the forehead. Then he took a deep breath and moved to the side so I could see Sam.

That first glimpse was startling: Sam was still under the effects of the paralytic, and he looked like a wax doll with one eye open.

"He looks so . . . still," I said.

"The paralytic should wear off soon," the nurse in the room said.

"Why is his eye open like that?"

"When the paralytic was given, he had one eye open. It will stay like that until the paralytic is out of his system."

"Good—because it is a little creepy."

As relieved as I was that the PDA was now closed and the surgery was over, the sight of Sam lying there motionless with one eye open and a big bandage on his back was really unsettling.

I stayed with Sam until Alison found us to tell me Dr. Kasahara was on the phone. I didn't need to fill her in, as Alison had given her the rundown. Dr. Kasahara told me my next steps were to have an ultrasound in the hospital and then come across the street to her office. She let me know the ultrasound tech was waiting, and the staff knew to bring me back the moment I got to her office.

As with the previous ultrasounds, the technician saw something still inside my uterus. Peter wheeled me across the street to Dr. Kasahara's office. We didn't even need to give our name when we walked in; they knew we were coming and had Peter wheel me right back to an exam room. Dr. Kasahara followed before we could even shut the door.

"Well, it looks like you still have some issues going on," Dr. Kasahara said as she sat down so we could be eye to eye.

"That is an understatement."

"The good news is I think this is all the result of a low-grade infection. I am going to put you on antibiotics. If you are still cramping and bleeding in three days, then we will schedule a D&C. I really want to avoid that if we can. You have been through enough."

Exhausted, tired in my bones, down a lot of blood, and on

heavy painkillers, I reluctantly agreed to go home and get some rest. My parents kept Irene an extra night, to spare her from seeing me looking so weak and to give me a chance to rest.

Between worry, my constant phone calls to the NICU, and the electronic baby, I didn't get a whole lot of sleep.

Chapter 29

Despite all the doctors' warnings about how bad Sam would get after the surgery, he did great. He had a little bit of trouble with his blood pressure at first, but, to help stabilize him, the doctors gave him several medications. By the time I called to check on Sam at 5 a.m., his blood pressure was under control and the doctors had taken him off two of the medications. By 9 a.m., they had taken Sam off the ventilator and put him back on SiPAP. When we arrived for a quick visit, Sam had been upgraded to CPAP. When we left not two hours later, the respiratory team was talking about starting Sam on cannula sprints again.

He was healing much faster than his mom was. Three days after Sam's surgery, I was finally starting to feel human. I was responding to the antibiotics, which meant a uterine infection might have been the cause of all my bleeding problems.

To celebrate our run of good news, Peter, Irene, and I went out for a family breakfast prior to heading over to the hospital. As with every weekend since Irene had announced she never wanted to go back to the NICU, I was going to be dropped off and Peter and Irene were going to head back home to hang out. As I was getting out of the car, Irene called out to me, "Mama, can I go with you to see Sam?"

I walked around to the back door, opened it, and knelt down. "Only if you want to, kiddo. There is no pressure."

"I really want to see him. He *is* my brother, you know," Irene said firmly.

"Well, then why don't you get out with me, and Daddy will go park the car."

Irene hopped out of the car, gave me a big hug, and held my hand while we waited for Peter to join us. Then, as a family, we headed in to see the little man.

Luckily my cousin Rosie, who is a child life specialist, had given us some advice and tips on how to make Irene feel safe in the NICU. First, she told us to wait for Irene to ask to see Sam. Her worry was that if we suggested it, Irene would feel pressured to say yes. We were to have no expectations about her visit, and we were to let her know she could leave at any time. Rosie also suggested we come up with a "safe" word or hand signal that Irene could use when she was ready to leave.

With Rosie's advice in mind, we talked to Irene before getting in the elevator.

"Remember, you can change your mind at any time, and we will not be mad," Peter started.

"And you can leave at any time you want," I added.

"I know. I really want to see him," Irene reassured us.

"How about we set a code word, OK? One that you can say, and Dad will know you are ready to leave."

"How about 'pickles'?" Peter suggested.

"I like 'pickles,'" Irene agreed.

With Irene reassured, the three of us headed into the NICU for our first full family visit in a few weeks.

Our excitement lasted until we walked into Sam's room and Evil Nurse greeted us. That's right. She was back and as awful as ever. She was rude to us, rude to Irene, and when my father arrived later, she was rude to him. I was sure that I had complained loudly enough to get this woman banned from Sam's care. I had talked to all the right people. And yet here she was. I knew I was going to have a very firm conversation with Misty to make sure this woman would never be near my family or me ever again.

Despite Evil Nurse's best efforts to deter her, Irene was excited to see Sam. We opened one of the doors on the isolette so Irene could talk to her brother.

"Hi, Sam. It's my birthday tomorrow! I wish you could be with me," she excitedly whispered. Then she held her hand up to Sam's open eyes and said, "Do you like my birthday nails?"

With those two things out of the way, Irene turned to her dad and said, "Pickles." We praised her for being such a big girl and wanting to visit her brother, and for being an even bigger girl by telling us when she'd had enough. I could tell by the look on Irene's face that she was feeling more comfortable about visiting Sam, which made my day.

After they left, I settled in for my Sammy cuddle time. As soon as Sam settled on my chest, he reached out to hold my hand. We sat there for about an hour, with Sam's hand wrapped around my thumb—relaxing as much as possible. It's amazing how much more secure I felt holding him this time. Since the surgery, he seemed much stronger. He rarely had apnea events, and his bradys were even less frequent. I didn't feel that I had to stare at the monitors watching his oxygen levels and his heart rate the entire time I held him. I could just relax and enjoy the moment.

Of course, Evil Nurse did her best to ruin the good cuddle at the end. Sam's CPAP machine started gurgling with water. Each time it made a sound, Sam would get startled and his oxygen levels would go down. I was unable to get the Evil Nurse's attention, and when I did, she was rude and unhelpful. The first thing she said when I finally called out her name was, "I'll put him back in a second."

Um, sorry, lady, that is not what I wanted. Perhaps next time, wait for the question!

I called out to her again, "Excuse me."

"I said I would put him back in a minute."

"Yeah. That's not what I am trying to ask you," I snapped. "The CPAP machine is gurgling and it is startling Sam. Can you drain it?"

She just walked away. By the time she came back five minutes later, Sam was totally agitated and we had to put him back in his isolette. My complaints about her this time would not just be her dismal attitude but her lackluster nursing skills.

When my dad arrived to pick me up, I was hot with anger toward this woman, and I really wanted to tell her off. I wanted her to know that the way she treated me and my family was unacceptable. I wanted her to understand that she made me not want to visit my own son. But I was also concerned that if I unleashed all of this anger and bile on her, she would then take it out on Sam. I could walk away, but Sam was stuck with her until the shift change. So I held my tongue and left as soon as my dad got there.

Besides, I had birthday cupcakes to make for Irene's class.

Chapter 30

Irene had been a big sister for thirty-two days when her fifth birthday rolled around. As a present, I decided to make this day "Irene Day." I would limit my time at the hospital and do whatever Irene wanted to do.

It was a school day, so Irene would be in class. That didn't stop Peter from taking the day off work. Just because Irene was in school didn't mean Mommy and Daddy wouldn't spend time in class with her. Oh no. I had made twenty-five vanilla cupcakes with buttercream frosting for her classmates, and I was going to be there to deliver them and watch the sugar crash in action.

But first, we'd sneak in a visit to the hospital.

When we got there, I immediately cornered Misty to talk about Evil Nurse. I didn't hold back this time, complaining about her attitude toward me and my family, as well as her attentiveness with Sam. I made it clear that I would not tolerate seeing her assigned to Sam again. Misty was very sympathetic and surprised that Evil Nurse was back with us, especially since I had previously asked for her to be banned. Being the great advocate that she was, Misty dug around until she found out what happened: somehow, Evil Nurse's name appeared on our primary list and not on our banned list. Misty also made sure the NICU nurse manager came over to talk to me so she could hear my complaints in person.

With that business out of the way, we went to see Sam. The first thing we noticed was the most amazing birthday card for Irene hanging from the IV pole next to Sam's isolette. Sam's night nurse, Lotte, had heard that it was Irene's birthday and helped Sam make a special card for his big sister. Cute little monkey stickers framed a card that said: "Happy Birthday, Sister! I Love You—Sam." The best part was the picture of Sam taken when Lotte changed Sam's NG tube, which can only be done by taking his nose cannulas off. So, for one blissful second, Sam's face was visible in all its glory. No tubes. No wires. Just his sweet squishy face. I wish Sam and Lotte could have seen Irene's smile when I brought her the card.

While we visited Sam, Teresa came in for a visit. She had been away the past week and was so happy to see how well Sam was doing.

"First thing I did when I got in this morning was to come take a look at Mr. Man," she told us. "I couldn't take my eyes off him. He looks so good and strong. It's amazing the difference."

"He is pretty great." I smiled.

"He is peeing! His skin color is amazing. His A's and B's are few and far between. And it looks like he has been weaned off most of the medications." She was rattling all this off so fast it was hard not to laugh.

"So, you're saying the surgery was a success?"

"Yes! Now we need to focus on Sam getting bigger so we can move him to the Fat Farm."

"The what now?"

"Nursery Three on the other side of the NICU, where babies go that just need to fatten up so they can go home," she responded.

Sam was still only two and a half pounds. To get the weight gain moving, Teresa doubled the amount of his feeds until he reached a target goal of 15 milliliters every feed, for a grand total of 120 milliliters every day, or half a cup.

We spent the rest of the day making Irene feel like the only kid in the world. Lord knows she deserved it. That past month had been so hard on her. She had started kindergarten, her mother had vanished without a word one afternoon, and she had this new tiny baby brother. We just wanted to make sure she felt special and loved.

We arrived at her school near the end of the day, and I guess word was out that cupcakes were coming because the whole class was already hyped up. Irene's poor teacher looked like he could not wait for the day to end. I guess birthdays in kindergarten are a teacher's worst nightmare. We handed out cupcakes, and the whole class sang "Happy Birthday." Our timing was perfect, because as soon as the kids ate the cupcakes and got the classroom cleaned up, the bell rang for the end of the day.

"You're coming with us," I said to Irene once everyone else had left the classroom.

"But why?" she asked, whining a little.

"Because we are spending the rest of the day with you," her dad answered.

"But they might be doing something for me in aftercare," Irene continued.

"OK. Poke your head in, say hi, then come meet us on the playground," I offered as a compromise.

Three minutes later, Irene came bounding out of aftercare ready for her adventure.

"So, we are at your mercy, kiddo. What would you like to do?" I asked.

"I wanna go to the park!" Irene squealed.

"Let's do it!"

We swung on swings, we slid down slides, we fed ducks, and we chased each other in circles. It was special behaving like a burden-free family, even for just a few hours. As much as Irene enjoyed herself, I think I may have enjoyed it more. Nothing can lift your spirits like acting like a little kid in the park on a sunny afternoon.

From there, we took Irene to the legendary Oakland ice cream parlor, Fentons, for an ice cream dinner. My family has always celebrated birthdays at Fentons, going back to when my mom was a little girl. While the inside of Fentons has changed over the years, the ice cream, the uncomfortable chairs with the wire heart backs, and the gigantic portion sizes remain the same. We got Irene's new year off on the right foot with a dinner of mac and cheese followed by a huge bowl of vanilla ice cream that was slathered in chocolate sauce. By the time we got home, we had succeeded in making Irene feel special, and in the process, we got to forget our troubles for just one day.

The following morning, Irene was still on a high from celebrating Irene Day. She bounded into our room first thing, crawled into bed, and snuggled up next to me.

"Can we make today Irene Day too?" she asked.

"I wish, kiddo," I laughed in response. "But I do have one surprise for you."

"What's that, Mama?" Irene asked, all excited.

"What would you think if I drove you to school today?" I asked.

While we were out celebrating Irene's birthday, Dr. Kasahara had left me a message letting me know that she was officially lifting my driving ban.

"YES!" I cheered.

After dropping Irene at school, I drove myself to the hospital.

Let me say that again: I drove myself to the hospital.

Sliding into the driver's seat for the first time in forty-three days and pulling out of my driveway made my heart race. I felt like an adult. I felt so free. I could go to the hospital when I wanted, leave when I wanted, come back if I wanted, even run errands if I wanted. What liberation! What a thrill!

Chapter 31

The next couple of days with Sam were boring—which, of course, was a good thing. He was growing. The only thing that changed with Sam was the amount of milk he was drinking and the resumption of cannula sprints.

I loved those sprints. Not only did I get to see Sam's handsome face, but I got to enjoy the sound of Sam breathing. I hadn't realized how loud the CPAP machine was. The sound would fill the room. After a while, I stopped noticing the noise, as it became part of my day-to-day life in the NICU. So, when Laura turned the CPAP off for the first time, the silence really stood out. In that silence, I listened to Sam breathe. It reminded me of when Irene was a newborn and I used to hold her in my arms, listening to her breathe. Now I could do that with Sam—just like any mom of a healthy newborn baby.

The first cannula sprint Sam did after his PDA ligation lasted over an hour. The next day, he sprinted again for an hour on a lower amount of oxygen. The next three days, he sprinted like a champ, each time lasting over an hour. Each time they lowered the oxygen a little more, until he was getting only a third of his oxygen through the cannula.

With all of these sprints, Sam was using more calories, as he had to actually work to breathe in enough air.

"Did you see the new orders Teresa left?" Laura asked me.

"No. Do I want to know?" I asked, afraid they might be bad news.

"Well, since Sam's is working so hard breathing, Teresa wants to up his milk intake."

"That is GREAT news!" I responded. "My freezer is overflowing with milk, and I am now storing milk at my parents' house." I laughed.

"Well, he is currently getting about seven milliliters every three hours. Tomorrow we will start to increase his feeds until Sam is up to fifteen milliliters every three hours for a grand total of one hundred and twenty milliliters every day."

"What is that in nonmedical terms?" I asked, having trouble picturing the amounts.

"About a half cup of milk a day," Laura told me.

Aside from allowing us to clear out some freezer space, the more milk Sam got, the faster the doctors could get him off the nutritional supplements in his PICC line, and then they could remove it. The PICC line, a long-term IV access, had been in place for over a month, and while it allowed Sam to get his nutritional supplements, it was also an infection risk. Getting this line out would drastically reduce this risk.

Of course, all this good news came with some bad news. The more Sam ate, the greater the risk of his bowels perforating, otherwise known as NEC. So far, Sam had managed to avoid it. I had spent the last thirty plus days holding my breath, terrified that one day Sam's intestines would fail. Now that the feeds were increasing so rapidly, that danger was becoming more of a reality.

Just as I had done for the past month, I had to push my fears aside and focus on the positives. I had to believe that everything was going to be OK. I had to have faith that the increase in feeds would not hurt Sam but would help him to grow bigger and stronger and eventually enable him to come home.

Chapter 32

When I first had a preemie, I didn't realize that feedings would be so impersonal. A feeding tube went down Sam's throat or nose, and the milk was delivered directly to his stomach with the push of a plunger on a syringe. Unlike the experience possible with a full-term baby, the chance of deep bonding through nursing was lacking. We were not nuzzled next to each other. The connection between milk and milk supplier was not there. Eating was passive. Sam didn't experience the sensation of a boob or even a bottle in his mouth.

Yes, I could hold Sam while the nurse pushed the milk into the feeding tube. But that is exactly as satisfying as it sounds.

This felt like one more thing that was taken away from me by Sam's prematurity. I had been denied the last sixteen weeks of my pregnancy. I had been denied the joy of feeling my baby move in my belly. I had been denied a normal birth experience. I had been denied that joy of leaving the hospital with my new baby. Now I was being denied the bonding of nursing my son.

Since the day Sam was born, I was determined to breastfeed. The lactation consultant, Deborah, warned me that the chances Sam would be able to nurse were slim, as many preemies never develop the ability to latch. I heard her; I just chose not to listen. Every day, I dreamed about Sam latching on to my breast and drinking up the milk I produced by the gallon. Teresa had told me the earliest I could expect Sam to latch was when he was thirty-two weeks gestational age (or eight weeks old). I had been watching the calendar, and knew we were getting close. I was excited and nervous. Despite my eagerness to put Sam to my breast, the thought that I would find out that he would not ever be able to nurse terrified me.

To prepare Sam for the possibility of breastfeeding, Deborah suggested I introduce him to my breast with recreational breastfeeding. Of all the terms and things I learned in the NICU, this one was hands down my favorite. It is the best description for what it is: while holding Sam, I was supposed to move him close to my nipple and let him smell it and maybe even lick it.

On Sam's thirty-sixth day of life, I asked if we could give recreational breastfeeding a try. Yes, he was only five weeks old, and yes, he only weighed two pounds, six ounces, but I was so desperate to see if he would respond. Laura could not think of a single reason why we should not try it. So, about an hour and a half into our cuddle, Laura helped me reposition Sam so his face was right at my nipple.

The first thing I did when we got in this position was confirm my suspicion that my nipples were currently bigger than Sam's mouth.

By quite a lot.

I guess not knowing how to latch wasn't the only thing keeping Sam from breastfeeding right now. There was no way he could open his mouth wide enough to get that nipple in.

After laughing about the size difference between my nipple and Sam's mouth, I just held my breath and watched Sam. At first, he was unhappy to be lying on his side and not upright on my chest. He squirmed around trying to get comfortable.

"Why don't you hand express some milk, so Sam can smell it," Laura suggested.

Once I did that, Sam started sniffing. Then he started to drool a little and smack his lips. And then out came his tiny tongue, and he started to lick up the little milk I had expressed. I would have been happy if he stopped there. But no. Not my Sam. He started trying to suck. He had a little piece of my nipple in his mouth, and that little bugger was sucking. He wasn't latched—as that would have been impossible with my gigantic nipples—but he was sucking. Laura was so impressed, she ran out to find Teresa and Deborah so they could see it too.

There the four of us were, all crammed into Sam's room, quietly staring at him trying to suck on a nipple the size of his entire head.

"Oh my God, Melissa. He's sucking!" Deborah exclaimed.

"I know!"

"Dr. Sandhu will not believe this," Teresa added

"I don't think I have seen a baby this young do this—ever," Deborah said.

"Really?" I asked. "So, do you think this means he will be able to breastfeed?"

"No guarantees, but this is really encouraging. My suggestion is you do this every time you hold Sam going forward."

"You don't have to tell me twice! I feel so motherly right now." I laughed.

And then I felt it. Hope. Real hope creeping in. Not only was my son going to be OK, but he was going to show everyone. He was going to breastfeed. He still had a long road ahead, but I just knew that my hope was not going to be misplaced.

Chapter 33

Since the first time I met Elisa in the NICU, I knew one day she and Bennett would finally be freed. She had spent so much time in the hospital prior to having Bennett due to her water breaking in her nineteenth week and then almost two months in the NICU after Bennett was born. Elisa and I often joked that it felt as if we had known each other for years, when it had only been thirtyish days. Kind of like dog years, NICU days count for more than their face value.

The end of Bennett's NICU stay was close at hand, and Elisa decided that before Bennett could leave, he needed to meet Sam. With the help of her nurse (who shall remain nameless to protect her), Elisa broke every NICU rule. She unhooked Bennett from all his monitors and walked him over to Sam's room for the boys' first ever playdate. She poked her head in while I had Sam on my chest for some kangaroo cuddle time.

"Hey," I said, "what are you doing over here? How is Bennett doing?"

"See for yourself," Elisa said as she fully entered the room with Bennett in her arms.

Laura took one look at Elisa. She laughed and said, "Um, you know you aren't supposed to do this, right?"

"What are you gonna do, throw us out?" Elisa asked.

Laura just shook her head and went back to what she was doing. "I hear nothing. I see nothing," she muttered under her breath.

"So, Bennett," Elisa said, "this is Sam. He is your first friend."

Following her lead, I whispered in Sam's ear, "And Sam, this is Bennett."

Not many kids can say they have been friends since they were fetuses . . . but these boys could.

The following day, Bennett and Elisa were liberated from the NICU. I was sad to see her go, but I was so excited for her. Plus, knowing that people do actually get to leave the NICU with beautiful, healthy babies gave me hope. Not having Elisa around the corner left a huge hole for me, but we still had Facebook and texting to keep us connected. Besides, once the boys were home, we were planning on a nanny share so we could keep the connection going.

After letting Sam coast for the past few weeks, Teresa had decided it was time to push Sam and set some big goals. The first goal was to get Sam digesting fifteen milliliters, or four teaspoons, per feed. Once he reached that goal, she was going to turn off the nutritional supplements Sam had received since he was born. Then the PICC line would be removed. Teresa also wanted Sam to go from one cannula sprint a day for two hours to three sprints a day for a grand total of six hours a day on the cannula.

Knowing that Teresa was going to push Sam, I sat down to give him a quick pep talk.

"Hi, baby. This is going to be a big week for you. Teresa wants to push you so you can come home as soon as possible. I need you to work hard and help us get you there. You are so strong and have amazed me so much already. I hate to ask you to push yourself harder, but I am. I know you can do it, baby. I know you can."

Pep talk over, I started chatting with Sam's evening nurse, Rochelle, and we came to the realization that Peter had yet to hold

Sam. His son was thirty-nine days old, and he still had not held him. To this day, I am mystified as to how this could have happened, but it did. Rochelle and I concluded that we had to put a stop to that silliness, and soon. I called Peter at work and told him to go straight to the hospital, and that Irene and I needed some bonding time.

Rochelle was ready for Peter the minute he walked in. Without even so much as a hello, Rochelle turned to Peter and said, "Unbutton your shirt and sit down."

Peter was thrown off guard and was unsure about what was going on, but he did what Rochelle told him. The next thing he knew, Rochelle was placing Sam on his chest for a little skin-to-skin daddy time.

When Peter got home later that night, his face said volumes. His eyes were a bit bloodshot and swollen but bright and brimming with joy.

"You OK?" I asked.

"There are no words."

"You liked it, then?"

"Yes. Thank you for arranging this. I almost didn't leave."

"You know, you can do it again, right? Just not when I am there."

"Ha ha. I know better than to get between you and your Sam cuddle time."

It was nice to see Peter looking so happy. I knew how relaxing and reassuring it was to hold Sam. Now he did too. The daddy/son connection had been expanded beyond changing a diaper and compassionate touch.

The next day, Sam digested the fifteen milliliters of milk and Teresa turned off the fat emulsion drip. Then she upped the goal to twenty milliliters per feed. When he got there, she promised to turn the HA solution off and take out the PICC line.

This run of boring days was starting to lull me into complacency. I was in a groove. Sam was trucking along, growing and wowing the doctors daily. In forty days, Sam had gained well over a pound and was just four hundred grams shy of doubling his birth weight to three pounds, eight ounces. With the increase in his feeds, he would do that in no time, and soon would be out of the two-pound weight class and up into the three-pound category.

I arrived at the hospital ready for another boring day filled with cannula sprints and recreational breastfeeding. Instead, I found Teresa in Sam's room, conferring with Laura and Dr. Sandhu. All three of them looked concerned. I slowed my pace down, just a little. It was clear something was wrong, and the longer it took for me to get there, the longer I could pretend everything was OK.

Teresa looked up and saw me. Her smile did nothing to calm me.

"Come on over, Melissa. We need to talk," Teresa said calmly.

"Can't I just pretend you aren't here?" I asked. "I liked the boring of the past few days."

"Wish you could, but we are concerned. Sam's stomach looks a bit distended."

Laura reached out her hand and put it on my shoulder.

"There could be a number of things causing this," Dr. Sandhu said.

"NEC is one them, isn't it?" I said with a totally defeated tone.

"NEC is just one of the things, yes," Dr. Sandhu confirmed—with an emphasis on the "just."

"We are going to get a stomach X-ray to see what is going on," Teresa added.

"Well, so much for boring," I said, slumping into the glider rocker next to Sam.

"How about we wait before we decide all is lost?" Laura added.

"You know me too well, Laura."

It took about thirty minutes for the portable X-ray machine to get to Sam's room. In that time, I just sat in the rocker, not talking, feeling all of the hope drain from my body.

We were talking about NEC.

NEC.

I had been having nightmares, both literal and figurative, about NEC. And now, here we were, worried that Sam had developed it. I tried not to go too far down the rabbit hole, but it was hard. The moment the X-rays arrived, Teresa and I huddled around the monitor and took a look. With a huge sigh of relief, Teresa turned to me and said, "It's not NEC. Your boy has gas!"

"Gas. All this is just gas. My God, he is his daddy's kid!" I yelled.

One possible side effect of being on CPAP is the buildup of air in the stomach. The only cure is to get the air out, and the best way to do that is to be held upright and patted. So I picked Sam up and settled into the rocker with him on my chest. The first twenty-five minutes I was holding him were very productive, with Sam farting up a storm.

The moment we put him back, we could see that he was fine. His stomach was back to normal.

Overnight Sam started to run a little fever, which led to concerns he might have an infection. It was also possible that his isolette was too warm, which meant Sam was getting overheated. To be safe, they changed out his isolette. In addition, they drew blood to check for infection and run a blood culture. It was a good thing they were cautious. While there was no sign of infection, his blood count was too low, which meant Sam needed another blood transfusion. Teresa was convinced this would be his last, and besides, he had responded so well to the previous transfusions, they didn't bother me anymore.

I sat with Sam while he got the transfusion, talking to him the entire time.

"I promise you, kiddo, once this is over, I am going to let you lick all the milk you want off my nipples. You just have to be patient."

As soon as the transfusion IV was removed, I picked Sam up and settled in. After about an hour, he started to fidget. Each time he wiggled, his oxygen levels would drop. He was wiggling a lot. Just as I was about to put him back, I realized he wasn't just wiggling, he was trying to get down to my nipple. I had promised him some recreational breastfeeding, and he was just trying to get me to follow through. Seeing as he was so eager, I repositioned him so his face was right by my nipple. Sam immediately started sniffing around and licking. Not happy to just lick, he tried to get my big old nipple into his little mouth. He managed to get a little in there, but that was not enough for him. Channeling a Muppet, Sam opened his mouth up wide enough and got the entire nipple in there. The next thing I knew, he was sucking . . . and sucking hard! My little thirty-weeker had latched! I doubt he was getting any milk, but he sure was trying. He sucked for thirty minutes. He could have gone longer, but I needed to pick up Irene from school.

It was clear to me that we needed Sam to get stronger so when he sucked, there was enough oomph behind it so he could actually get milk.

The following day, still riding the high of getting a full nipple in his mouth, Sam ticked off a few more goals on Teresa's list, and she was able to turn the supplements off and remove the PICC line.

But that wasn't enough for my man. Oh no. Sam had been doing so well on his cannula sprints, the respiratory team decided to take him off CPAP full-time.

"Are you telling me that the cannulas are staying in full-time?" I asked Teresa.

"Well, until he is ready to be off them as well," she answered. "As with anything here, however, you know he may have to go back on the CPAP."

"I know, I know. Nothing is a guarantee in the NICU," I responded. "Who do you think I am . . . a newbie?"

"Good point," Teresa laughed as she left Sam's room.

My little six-week-old baby was officially breathing on his own (with an assist of oxygen through a cannula). The joy of that news was nothing compared to the joy of seeing more of Sam's face. The CPAP machine used a mask that covered Sam's nose and partially obscured his eyes. Now I could take in all the glory of his cute little nose all the time. I knew this could change, but for now, I drank it all in. After four days, the CPAP machine was removed completely from Sam's room. He wasn't going back.

Chapter 34

The next two weeks were so wonderful. Every day I went to the NICU to visit, and every day, Sam was a totally normal, if small, baby. The only excitement we had was on Sam's forty-seventh day in the NICU. As I arrived in his room and lifted back the quilt covering his isolette, I discovered that Sam had removed his feeding tube. It was the first time since he was born that I got to see his mouth with nothing in it. He really did have a beautiful mouth, and his daddy's lips.

Sam looked so proud of what he had accomplished. I would say he even looked smug. Teresa and Laura had a quick chat and decided that Sam's nose was big enough that we could try putting the tube in through his nose as opposed to in his mouth. That sounded good to me as I would get to see more of his face and Sam couldn't remove the feeding tube by drooling.

After some skin-to-skin time, I placed Sam back in his isolette.

"Hey, Laura, do you think we could play dress-up with Sam?"

Up until now, Sam had never worn anything but a diaper and a blanket. Now that his PICC line was out, and only the monitor lines, cannula, and feeding tube were left, putting him in some cute preemie clothes was possible.

"I can't think of a reason why not," Laura said with a smile. "Let's do it."

Oh.

My.

God.

Playing dress-up with Sam was the highlight of my month. Sam was so damn cute in his green-and-yellow striped onesie. Even though it was a preemie-sized onesie, it was huge on Sam. But I didn't care. With clothing on, Sam looked even more like a baby, not just a preemie.

As much fun as playing dress-up was for me, Laura told me it was also an important developmental activity. For the life of me I couldn't figure out how that could be true, but I didn't care.

Now that Sam was a big boy, wearing clothes and breathing pretty much on his own, it was time for him to get his first vaccinations. The state of California requires all babies, regardless of gestational age, to be vaccinated for pertussis by the sixth week of life. This seems like an oversight in the law; Sam wasn't even supposed to be born for another ten weeks, how could he need a vaccination? Regardless, Sam was a total trooper with the needle. He didn't even flinch when the nurse gave him the shot. Of course, the preemie "anesthetic" he was given may also have played a part.

In the NICU, nurses and doctors use sugar water in the mouth as an anesthetic. A few drops on the tongue before a shot and some babies, including Sam, are so blissed out, they don't even notice. It's a shame that the sugar anesthetic effect doesn't last forever. Imagine how much easier shots or blood draws would be if you could have some sugar water before the shot and not feel a thing.

After his shots, Sam slept most of the rest of the day away, which gave me time to talk with Teresa about when Sam would graduate from Nursery Two to Nursery Three—where babies go to fatten up before being released.

"When will Sam move to the Fat Farm?" I asked.

Teresa laughed. "Ah, the Fat Farm. We are getting closer to that day, but not quite yet."

As exciting as it was to think of Sam going to the Fat Farm, I was still worried. We had had such good juju in Nursery Two. Plus, the last time they moved us from this part of the NICU, it was not a good experience.

"OK. But I'm curious, when Sam does move, will Laura go with him?" I asked.

There was no way I would allow Sam to leave Laura at this point. It wasn't so much that Sam needed her; *I* needed her. I spent more time with Laura than any other adult. She was there to buck me up, hold my hand, make me laugh, and provide me with adult conversation.

"At this point, wherever Sam goes, Laura goes," Teresa assured me.

"Damn straight," Laura chimed in from Sam's room. Apparently, she had heard our conversation.

"Is there any way to request a particular room in the Fat Farm?" I asked.

"You are a longtimer—you can ask for whatever you want," Teresa responded.

"I believe in NICU juju. I would love it if we could get Bennett's old spot," I told her.

"Juju and a view," Teresa teased. "No promises, but when the time comes, we will do our best to get you that spot."

To celebrate his fiftieth day in the NICU, Sam took recreational breastfeeding to a new level. As he had been doing the past week or so, he latched on right away, but this time he started sucking so hard, milk came out and he was actually swallowing. He was getting so much milk, I could hear him gulping.

"Melissa, is that Sam swallowing?" Laura asked.

"Yes! Oh my God. Yes!"

"I'm getting Teresa!"

Moments later, Teresa arrived with Blanca, the other nurse practitioner in the NICU.

"I win!" Teresa said, looking at Blanca.

"No way," Blanca replied.

"Yes way. My twenty-four-weeker is a breast feeder!" Teresa beamed. (I loved that she called Sam hers.)

Just then, Sam took a huge gulp that all of us could hear.

"Shit. Fine. You win," Blanca said with a smile.

"Would one of you care to explain?" I asked.

"Blanca and I had a little competition going," Teresa started.

"I have a former twenty-four-weeker over in Nursery Two who is two weeks older than Sam," Blanca added.

"She made the mistake of thinking her kiddo would breast-feed before Sam," Teresa chimed in. "Everyone here knows never to bet against Sam."

Teresa was beaming with pride. I couldn't help but join her. I loved her confidence in Sam, and that she had won her bet.

The next day when I came to see my little overachiever, I beamed with pride again as the little breastfeeding machine had finally moved out of the two-pound weight class and joined the three-pound class. He was starting to get little fat jowls around his face. He'd worked hard for those jowls, and I loved every bit of them.

When I called home to tell everyone how fat Sam was getting, Irene grabbed the phone.

"Mama, I want to come see Sam again!" she shouted.

"If you're sure, I think he would love that. Remember, all you have to say is 'pickles,' and Dad will take you home."

Peter and Irene arrived just as I was settling in to breastfeed Sam. Irene lit up when she saw Sam in my lap. This was the first time she had ever seen him outside of the isolette. Plus, with Sam off of CPAP and the PICC line removed, he was looking a lot less scary.

"Wow. Mom. Sam looks like a real baby!" Irene said. "Can I touch him?"

"Did you wash your hands really good before coming in here?" I asked.

"Of course, Mama. Dad timed me."

"Then just be really gentle and go for it."

Irene got really close and put her hand on Sam's head.

"Hi, baby brother," she said over and over.

Irene then reached down to Sam's hand, and as soon as her fingers got there, he grabbed her and held on. Irene smiled and giggled.

I began to cry.

Here I was, nursing my son while he and my daughter held hands. Irene noticed my tears, which confused her.

"Why are you crying, Mama?"

"I am happy."

"Me too. I like Sam. He isn't scary anymore."

And she was right. He really wasn't scary anymore. He was over three pounds. There were no loud machines breathing for him. He had no wires or tubes in him. He was even wearing clothes. I wiped my tears away, gave my girl a kiss, and smiled.

"Why are you smiling, Mama?"

"I am happy."

"You're funny, Mama."

Chapter 35

Fifty-nine days after rolling into the NICU, Sam was promoted to Bennett's old spot in Nursery Three. We were finally in the Fat Farm, where Sam's only job was to eat, get fat, learn to regulate his body temperature, and breathe without the cannula.

One of the great benefits of Sam's new spot was the huge window with a sweeping view of the Berkeley Hills. I had been in the NICU for so long, deprived of natural light, that my solar-powered watch had stopped working.

As much as I loved the natural light, the large window also meant that Sam finally got to feel the sun on his face for the first time. Seeing him bathed in sunlight was wonderful. It's hard to imagine spending fifty-nine days of your life never knowing the joy of napping in a sunbeam. I made sure to explain to Sam what he was feeling so he wouldn't be scared. Of course, the moment Sam got in the sun, he sighed and continued to sleep, never opening his eyes. I swear he had a smile on his face and slept a little more soundly in that sunbeam.

The following day, the sun was pouring into Sam's room, bathing his isolette in light. Laura had a quilt covering the isolette. The last thing we wanted was for Sam to get overheated or a sunburn.

I pulled the quilt back and found Sam sleeping soundly with his nose cannula sitting outside his nostrils on the bridge of his nose. I glanced up at the monitors just to see his oxygen levels, which were at 97 percent. I was about to put the cannula back, but I stopped myself. I decided to just watch and see what would happen.

The next ten minutes I sat there, keeping my secret, watching the monitor. Sam's numbers fluctuated between 95 and 99. I could hear Teresa in the next room.

"Hey, Teresa, when you have a moment," I called out.

"Everything OK?" she asked.

"Yep. Just had a quick question."

I didn't want to tell her about my experiment. If she knew he was breathing on his own, she would make me put the cannula back.

"How's my man today?" Teresa asked.

"Look at the monitor. See his oxygen levels?"

"They look great."

Now I started to smile.

"I know."

"Melissa . . . what are you up to?" Teresa asked.

"Look at Sam's face."

She glanced down and saw the cannula on the bridge of his nose.

"He's been like this for fifteen minutes." I beamed.

Now, here I was thinking I was being so daring letting Sam do this test without Teresa or anyone knowing. I was sure she would tell me that it was too soon, and she would put the cannula back in his nose.

"Oh. I guess he's ready to be done with the cannula," Teresa said, all matter-of-fact. And with that, she turned the oxygen off, smiled at me, and left the room.

With no fanfare, Sam was off the cannula.

If Sam being taken off oxygen wasn't enough to make my day,

his afternoon nurse was also the lead NICU discharge specialist.

"Well, he keeps going like this," she said, "he will be home in three to fours weeks."

Holy crap!

My imprisonment in the NICU suddenly had an end in sight—and it was closer than I ever could have imagined.

Chapter 36

Having a baby in the NICU is so hard on a parent. You feel helpless when it comes to caring for your child. As a mom, there is all this guilt on top of the feelings of helplessness. For me, I channeled all of those feelings into my milk supply. I felt that I may have let Sam down when it came to gestation, but the least I could do was produce enough milk for him.

In just a few short days, it became clear that milk was not going to be a problem for me. Now, two months after Sam was born, my milk supply was in overdrive. I diligently recorded how much milk I produced each time I pumped. I was averaging two thousand milliliters a day (a little over eight and a half cups); the target amount was only one thousand milliliters (about four cups) a day. I had milk stored in every possible freezer available to me: the hospital, our large stand-up freezer, a small freezer I had purchased just to hold milk, my parents' freezer, and the bottom drawer of the freezer in our kitchen. I had enough milk to feed triplets for months.

Knowing how full all the freezers were, I decided to calculate how much milk I had pumped since Sam was born. I went through all of my logs, tallied it up, and was dumbfounded to see I had pumped 3,174 ounces, or 24.7 gallons, of milk.

In two months.

When I got to the NICU, I found Deborah and filled her in on my milk tally.

"So, I have pumped like twenty-four gallons of milk."

She said nothing. Her mouth was open just a little.

"Is that . . . normal?" I asked.

"Good God no. That is more than you should be producing for a term baby," Deborah said. "Sam will never be able to drink all of that before it expires."

"Frozen milk expires?" I asked.

"Oh yes. Depending on the freezer, anywhere from six months to a year. But you already have a huge supply and are still adding to it."

"What do I do with the milk then?" I asked. The last thing I wanted to do was let it go to waste.

"Donate it!"

Deborah put me in touch with the Mother's Milk Bank based in San Jose, California. This is an amazing organization that collects breast milk, pasteurizes it, and sends it out to local hospitals to be given to preemies who, for whatever reason, do not have access to breast milk. They also sell a portion of their milk to moms who need it for their babies, which in turn helps fund the free milk they provide to NICU babies.

I loved the idea that my overabundance would go to help other preemies.

I called the milk bank, filled out the donor application, went through all the testing, and arranged my first donation. Once I was cleared, a volunteer drove to my house and collected about two thousand ounces of milk. This opened up a huge space in my freezer and made me feel great.

I would make two more donations to the milk bank, for a grand total of five thousand ounces, or about forty gallons.

Chapter 37

N ow that Sam was off the cannula, there were only two more milestones to pass before he could come home: he had to maintain his own body temperature, and he had to take all of his feedings either from the breast or the bottle.

Sam was well on his way with the feedings, latching to the boob most of the time. I had not allowed the nurses to give him a bottle. I wanted to be absolutely sure that Sam would prefer the breast to the bottle. Until he latched every time the boob was offered to him, I was not ready to let him have a bottle.

As for his body temperature, the only way we would know if Sam was able to hold his temperature was to move him from an isolette to an open crib. So, sixty-six days into his NICU stay, Laura made up an open crib for Sam and moved him from the comfort of the isolette to the "fresh air" of the open crib.

I loved this move. With Sam out of the isolette, I could put my hands on him without having to open doors. Plus, the open crib made it easy to kiss him whenever I wanted. And I could just lean over and pick my boy up.

With Sam now out in the open, I suggested my parents pick Irene up from school and bring her by the hospital. I didn't tell them what I was planning, but I made it clear that it would be worthwhile.

They arrived a little after four with Irene. She was so excited to see Sam out in the open. She beamed at me and said, "Mama, I can touch him without any help!" I just smiled at her and asked her to sit down.

"Why, Mama?"

"Honey, please, just sit."

She did, but she scrunched her nose up at me and let out a loud huff. Irene does not like being told what to do. I asked my mom to put the breastfeeding pillow in Irene's lap. Now my mom was confused. I could see my dad's face change as he figured out what I was up to. He gave my mom a quick elbow and then smiled at her. You could see she was getting it. Irene, on the other hand, was still clueless.

Mom put the pillow in Irene's lap. Before Irene could start to complain again, I picked Sam up from the crib and placed him in her lap.

I didn't build it up; I didn't make a big deal out of it. I just placed her brother in her lap.

Irene looked at her brother and then at me, and then at her brother, and then back to me. I could see my dad wiping a tear from his eyes. My mom and I were less composed. We both had tears streaming down our faces. I think Laura even shed a tear or two.

Irene giggled and smiled. She sat there, perfectly still, holding her baby brother.

"Can I kiss him?" Irene asked after a few minutes.

"Of course, kiddo."

Irene leaned down, buried her face in his forehead, and covered him with kisses.

My dad was ready for the moment and had the camera all set. He captured two perfect pictures of Irene and Sam. In the first, Irene has a huge toothy smile on her face. Her big blue eyes are sparkling as she looks at the camera. Her golden brown curls framed her face and tickled Sam's forehead. Sam is wrapped up in a hospital blanket, lying on his back facing Irene. He looks like he has a smile on his face. The next one Dad managed to get is even better than the first. In this one, Irene has leaned down and is gently kissing her brother on the forehead. Sam has opened his eyes and is staring right at his big sister.

I texted both pictures to Peter, who was just about to get in his car and head home. He told me that he sat in his car and wept for a few minutes before starting the drive. He said they were the most beautiful pictures he had ever seen.

The following day was Thanksgiving, and I had so much to be grateful for. I had the love and support from friends and family. The amazing staff at Alta Bates hospital, who had not only helped me make it through six days in Trendelenburg but also worked the past two-plus months to keep Sam safe and healthy. There was Irene, whose spirit and joy are contagious. Most of all there was Sam. I was so grateful for him and his strength of spirit.

Chapter 38

Things had been good for so long, I almost forgot that the NICU was a roller coaster, where things can take a turn for the worse at any moment.

Sam had been in the open crib for a few days and was having a hard time maintaining his body temperature. Teresa moved Sam away from the window to a spot with less of a draft. I had never noticed the draft, but Teresa convinced me it was there. While this wasn't a big setback, I had fought for this window space, and I really didn't like the idea of giving it up.

Besides, this wasn't just Sam's room; this was also my home away from home. In the NICU, I didn't have control over much, so ever since Sam was moved that first time, I took it upon myself to control where Sam was located. I fought to keep him in Room 11 until he was ready to move to the Fat Farm. Then I fought to get him Bennett's old spot. Now Teresa was telling me that I had to give that spot up. I knew it was for the right reasons, but it still really bothered me.

I was already on edge, and things went downhill from there. Dr. Stern, the pediatric ophthalmologist, arrived to give Sam his scheduled eye exam. This was Sam's third eye exam. Each showed that Sam had premature eyes (duh). The doctors were watching his eye development closely to make sure Sam was not developing retinopathy of prematurity (ROP).

I had never been present when Dr. Stern was in the NICU. This time, I was able to ask him to help me understand ROP better.

"I know that ROP is common in premature babies, but I still don't fully understand what it is," I said.

"ROP affects the growth of the blood vessels of the retina and, if left untreated, can cause the retina to detach, resulting in permanent blindness," Dr. Stern explained.

This, I understood.

"How bad is this? Is Sam in danger of going blind?" I asked, catching a little in my throat.

"The ROP is getting worse. I am calling in a specialist to examine Sam."

This development put our looming discharge date in doubt. Not that anyone had guaranteed us we would in fact go home on a certain date, but we had been moving steadily in that direction, and I had built it up in my head as a fact. So, when the ROP showed up, the realization that Sam would not be going home in the next two weeks slapped me in the face.

Seeing that I was starting to go to a dark place, Laura gave me a kind smile, put her arm around my shoulder, and said, "Go home."

"I don't want to go home," I snapped back at her.

She gave me a look. "Girl. You need to go home and digest this news. Until the specialist comes, we will not really know anything. Take care of you. Crack open a bottle of wine and wallow."

It was clear she was not asking; she was telling.

I decided to listen, if just for one night.

I followed Laura's advice, but it didn't help. The next day I was in even more of a funk. Everything got to me. I was mad I had gotten my hopes up about Sam coming home. I was mad at not being in the window spot. I was mad at Sam for not latching every time I tried to feed him. I was mad at Sam for not maintaining his body temperature. I was mad at Sam for still having bradys. (I knew Sam would not be allowed to go home unless he had been brady free for five straight days.) I was mad at the retina specialist for not dropping everything and coming to see Sam. I was mad at the hospital cafeteria for failing to put out kidney beans in the salad bar every day.

I was just mad.

My foul mood continued for days.

It got so bad, one day I threw a total tantrum in the NICU. I snapped at Laura for no reason. I was snotty to Teresa for failing to pressure the retina specialist into seeing Sam. I actually yelled at the charge nurse for not moving us back to the window spot despite the fact that Sam couldn't hold his body temperature. I had reached my breaking point and I was acting like a petulant child. It's not that anything in particular set me off. I was just so over the NICU. I loved the people in the NICU, but for fuck's sake, I was just over it.

I hated the parking garage. I hated the constant alarms. I hated the lack of privacy. I hated the lack of control.

I just wanted my boy home—and I had no idea when that would happen.

Sam was still not latching and breastfeeding consistently. We knew he could latch, but there were days when all he would do is lick my nipples and fall asleep. I was still not allowing the nurses to introduce the bottle, which meant Sam was still relying on a tube going down his nose into his stomach for feeds. Until he was getting all his food from me or a bottle, he would not be allowed to go home. So we had ourselves a bit of a standoff.

And just when I thought my dark mood couldn't get any worse, the retina specialist finally came to examine Sam—and let me tell you, it was not pleasant to watch. First, they put drops in

Sam's eyes to dilate them. He screamed. Then they put in another set of drops to numb the eyeball. He screamed again. Then the doctor pulled the upper and lower eyelids back and held them in place with some wacky-looking tongs. The screams got louder and Sam started to flail, so Laura had to hold him down. With Sam's eyelids pried open, the doctor used a little probe and a beam of light to look into his eyes. I kept my eyes fixed on Sam's heart rate monitor. I figured the less I saw, the better.

When the exam was over, the doctor turned to me.

"Your son has stage four ROP in both eyes."

"Is that good or bad?" I asked.

"It is as bad as we can let it go without there being permanent damage."

"You mean blindness?"

"Yes. He needs surgery."

I took a deep breath in. "What does this surgery look like?"

"I will come in, and with a specialized laser stop the development of the abnormal blood vessels."

"And that is done here?" I asked.

"Yes. It will take around two hours."

"And you are sure?" I asked. "He has been through so much."

"Without the surgery, your son will go blind."

I nodded and began to cry.

Since Sam's eyes were getting worse every day, we scheduled the surgery for the first available date, three days after the diagnosis. This gave me a few days to convince myself that Sam would be blind otherwise, cry a bunch, get over it, and come back out the other side to the world of positive thinking. I had to have faith in this retina specialist. He was supposed to be one of the best in the country—so that should count for something.

Chapter 39

The day before Sam was scheduled for surgery, we got a phone call at about 9:30 p.m. This was the first time in a long time that the NICU had called us. I knew that something must be wrong. There was no other reason for the NICU to call.

Since I had left earlier that day, Sam had been slowly declining. It started with him having residuals, or undigested food, in his stomach after a feed. He should instantly digest milk when being fed through a feeding tube. Nurses can check this by suctioning the feeding tube. If nothing comes up, then all the food has been digested. If milk comes back up, that is a residual.

As the day progressed, the amount of residuals got bigger and bigger. With less food in his system, Sam became lethargic. This was enough to concern the neonatologist on duty. His concern concerned me. He suspected that Sam might have another infection, so he ordered blood work and a chest X-ray.

It had been so long since Sam worried a doctor this much. The doctor's concern got me all worked up. After I hung up the phone, I turned to Peter and said, "I am going to the hospital."

"I understand. What time will you be back?" he asked.

"I don't think you understand. I will not be leaving. I am going to spend the night in the NICU with Sam."

~

By the time I arrived, Sam's condition had declined further. He had respiratory problems, and had one apnea event that required vigorous stimulation to get him to breathe again. Things got so bad, the respiratory team put Sam back on the nose cannula. As a precaution, the neonatologist also placed an IV for fluids and antibiotics.

Because of Sam's precarious condition, he needed to be moved out of Nursery Three back to Nursery Two. This was a big deal, because it meant that he was no longer considered stable and needed more hands-on monitoring.

We were lucky enough to get an entire room to ourselves.

"Would it be possible to set up a cot for me in here?" I asked. "Otherwise, I can just sleep in the rocker."

"Yeah, we can make that work."

It turned out to be an unnecessary request. I never even had a chance to get in bed.

Sam was really struggling. Every few minutes an alarm would go off signaling Sam's plummeting respiration rate and oxygen levels.

Sam's nurse and I would jump in and work to stimulate Sam back to breathing.

"Come on, kiddo. You gotta breathe," I would tell him.

Sometimes that would work. Other times we would need to rub his chest or gently pinch his heels.

It went on like this all night. Each time the alarm went off my heart would sink. He had done so well for so long, to see him have such a terrifying setback was demoralizing. I felt each alarm as a punch in the gut. That night, I was punched a lot.

By the time morning came around, I was exhausted and on edge. I was worried that this setback would delay the eye surgery, which would delay his release, which would keep me stuck in the NICU forever.

Luckily, the retina specialist and Dr. Sandhu talked and decided that Sam was strong enough for the surgery and scheduled it for that night.

Sam had a hard time all day, suffering a number of apnea and brady events. Peter took the day off of work, and he and I both did our best to comfort him, taking turns holding him and talking to him. My parents arrived at the hospital around 5:30 p.m. with dinner. Sam's nurse convinced us to take a break and eat something. He also needed us to clear the room so he could get it ready for the surgery.

Unlike the PDA surgery, the room didn't need to be made into a sterile operating room. Instead, the room needed to be completely dark, so every window and door was covered with special paper to ensure a complete blackout.

After dinner Mom, Dad, Peter, and I all hung around Sam's isolette. The surgery was set for 7 p.m. By 7:30 p.m., we all started to get a little agitated. By 10 p.m, the surgeon still had not arrived.

"I can't take this, Melissa. I am going to talk to someone," my dad announced.

"Dad. This isn't like your entrée is taking too long to come out," I said. "We just have to wait."

"He's got five more minutes, then I am finding someone," Dad huffed as he sat back down.

Luckily, Dad didn't get a chance to make a stink, as no sooner had Dad sat down than the surgeon walked in.

Just like Paladin from the TV show *Have Gun—Will Travel*, the doctor came striding in with his tools in a black case. He said very little to us, just went into Sam's room and shut the door. About an hour and a half later, he came out, told us it went well, and vanished into the night. We quickly named him Paladin, and to this day, that is what we call him.

In the time he was with Sam, Paladin used a laser to create a clean ridge to which the retina could attach. We would have to wait a few days to get preliminary results and then have Sam checked a number of times over the next few months before we would know for sure if the surgery was a success. The confidence the NICU staff had in Paladin and his success rate filled me with hope.

After Paladin left, Mom, Dad, and Peter came in to see Sam. He was sleeping and his eyes were red and swollen. After a few words of love, they left and I settled in for another night in the NICU.

That night, as with the previous night, Sam had trouble keeping his heart rate and oxygen levels up. Some of the events were so bad, he required rough stimulation to get back to normal numbers. I maybe got an hour of sleep in two days, but I was so glad I was there with him. By the time morning rolled around, Sam had settled down, and the number and severity of A's and B's had diminished.

Unfortunately, even though Sam was doing better, the sleep deprivation and stress of the past few days exacerbated my terrible mood. Little things now seemed like major problems. I was taking new developments much harder and having a hard time seeing a possible end to our NICU stay. Some of it had to do with the fact that just a few weeks ago, we were talking about this being the week we were going home. Now nobody was talking to us about a new go-home date.

I started thinking about all the hurdles that lay ahead of Sam. Not just the hurdle of getting out of the NICU. No, I started thinking about what possible challenges lay ahead for us once he was home. Would Sam have any major disabilities? Would he be able to hear? See? Would he have cerebral palsy? Would he have major developmental delays? Would he have any quality of life? I was unable to stay in the present. Now I felt more and more like I was slipping into the dark side of being a NICU mom, wherein every little setback (real or perceived) sent me into a tailspin, convinced that there was something terribly wrong.

Sam was taking a long time to wake up from the sedatives from the surgery. The doctors were starting to get concerned. Then, once he finally woke up, he started having large amounts of undigested milk again after each feed. Those two things together set me further down the worry path.

On top of all that was the fact that Sam wasn't crying. I knew it was crazy to complain that my baby wasn't crying a lot, but in this case, I felt as if it was an ominous sign of something being wrong.

Luckily, Laura had come on duty. She walked into the room, took one look at me, and shook her head.

"Nope. That's not going to work," she said.

"What's not?" I snapped at her.

"You and that attitude. You look like hell, and I can see in your eyes that you are not in the right headspace to be here," she said emphatically. "You can choose to go home and nap, or I can kick you out and you can go home and nap."

I was about to tell her she was not my boss, but Laura stared me down, as if she was daring me to argue.

"Fine. But don't think I am going to let you push me around every time you don't like my mood."

"I would expect nothing less," Laura said before giving me a big hug and promising me that she would call if anything, good or bad, happened.

After a solid night of sleep, my dad took me to the hospital the next day.

"I wanted to drive you so we could talk."

"What did I do now?" I asked. It's never good when your dad wants to talk.

"You haven't been yourself lately. I am worried you are not taking care of you."

"I don't know how to take care of me right now, Dad. My job is to take care of Sam."

"No. Your job is to take care of you so you can take care of Sam—and Irene." Dad added the "and Irene" after he put a gentle hand on mine.

"I'm just tired. I promise. I will try and not spend a long time here today. OK?"

"You don't have a choice," my dad said, smiling. "I drove you here."

Luckily, when we arrived we found Sam squirming, alert, and hungry. With very little effort, I was able to get Sam to latch and power down some breast milk right from the source. With each gulp, I felt my positivity returning.

Chapter 40

Less than three days after the eye surgery, Sam was off the cannula and the IV and he was back in Nursery Three. We were not in the window spot yet; Sam was still having trouble with his body temperature. But at least we were back in Nursery Three. Laura and I had a pact to move Sam back to that window just as soon as he was ready.

Not wanting to put Sam back in an isolette, Laura hunted down the one heated open crib in the NICU. The crib looked like it had been made in the late sixties. We named it the "Easy Bake Oven," as the heating element was a big light bulb under the mattress.

Having Sam in the Easy Bake Oven really helped, and within two days, we were able to make our last move in the NICU—back to the window spot. Laura assured me that this would be the last move before the big move of taking Sam home.

Now that Sam was through the surgery and was digesting his food, Teresa, Laura, Dr. Sandhu, and I turned our attention to getting Sam home in time for Christmas. We had the next sixteen days to ensure that Sam was getting all of his nutrition from the breast or the bottle, that his body temperature was stable, and that he was brady free for five straight days.

The easiest of these hurdles was the issue of body temperature.

As Sam gained more weight, his temperature stabilized. By now, he was spending most of the daytime in the non-heated open crib. He only had to go into the Easy Bake Oven at nighttime. To give him a little extra boost, I purchased every fleece preemie footie pajama I could find online—three, to be exact. The hope was the extra warmth from the clothing would be what finally enabled him to graduate from the Easy Bake Oven.

As for the feeding, the lactation consultant, Deborah, finally convinced me to introduce the bottle. Sam had already proven he could breastfeed, and with my overactive supply, she was not worried that he would opt for bottle over boob. She also told me that introducing the bottle would improve Sam's breastfeeding.

I got her logic: by using a bottle, Sam would learn that he had to suck to get food, which would then increase his instinct to suck. Also, with a bottle, Sam didn't have a choice on how much he could eat. It was decided for him. With the breast, he could eat as much as he wanted, which would make the breast more desirable. Finally convinced, I agreed to introduce the bottle.

As happy as Deborah was with my decision, Laura was thrilled.

"About damn time, Melissa," she said with a huge smile.

"Why is this such a big deal for you?" I asked.

"Who do you think is going to get to hold and feed Sam?" Laura answered.

It really hadn't even occurred to me that, up to that point, Laura very rarely got to pick Sam up and just hold him. Now she would get to have some special bonding time with her favorite boy.

My mom, who was with me that day, elbowed me and said, "I'm with Laura on this."

"*Et tu*?" I laughed.

"You don't think I want a chance to feed my grandson?"

It was a win-win for everyone.

~

We had a discharge goal. We had a plan on how to get there. We had sixteen days left. It didn't seem like a long time, but those last days in the NICU felt as if they dragged on forever. Each day that passed without a medical crisis or a brady was marred by this black cloud of fear that hung over me. I was convinced something would happen that would keep us trapped in the NICU longer. Each of Sam's nurses tried to encourage me and help me focus on all of the good news we were getting. I just had a hard time not letting my fears overshadow the good news. I was depressed, angry, and tired of being a NICU mom. Every little setback, like a brady or Sam's body temperature not staying high enough, felt like Armageddon. My anger made it hard to enjoy even the good days.

When Paladin came back and examined Sam after his eye surgery, he told me, "I would be shocked if things took a turn for the worse." Laura assured me that this meant Sam's retinas were nicely attached and should stay that way. Or, in other words, no blindness for my little man. He may have some vision issues, but some vision issues are way better than blindness. I was happy that things looked good, but since Paladin didn't say specifically that Sam would not be blind, I was unable to rejoice. I was sure something bad was coming.

When we introduced the bottle for the first time, Sam latched on to it and sucked the milk down like a pro. Again, my first thoughts weren't that this was good news. My first thought was "Great, now he is going to want the bottle more than the boob." Of course, he latched onto the boob as easily as he latched onto the bottle, but I was sure this was the beginning of the end of the breastfeeding. Of course I was wrong, as Sam didn't fully wean until he was more than two years old.

~

Even though it felt like every day was taking forever, the reality was Sam was progressing quickly. He was officially out of the Easy Bake Oven. He was going two to three days at a stretch without having a brady. And he was taking most of his food by either breast or bottle. Sam was so consistent that on his eighty-seventh day in the NICU, the nurses removed his feeding tube for the last time. Dr. Sandhu even pulled me aside and told me that as long as Sam went five days without a brady, he would be coming home.

Irene, on the other hand, had a terrible couple of days. Right in the height of flu and respiratory syncytial virus (RSV) season, Irene got sick. She spiked a high fever and could not hold down food. Her timing was terrible. With Sam off the feeding tube, I was at the hospital for at least three of his feeds every day.

"Peter!" I yelled, waking him up one morning.

"What . . . what's wrong?" he asked.

"Christmas is in a few days," I said.

"And?" Peter asked.

"And . . . we don't have a tree. We can't not have a tree for Irene."

Peter was now fully awake and aware of the situation.

"OK. Here's what we do. Let's see if your parents can take care of Irene, you and I will go to the hospital together, and after you feed Sam, we will get a tree."

I was remarkably shocked with how rational and easy the plan Peter suggested was.

With a sick Irene tucked in happily at my parents' house, Peter and I headed to the hospital. We arrived just in time for Sam's 9 a.m. feed. Sam nursed like a champ, and we told the nurse we would be back for the 12 p.m. feed, after running a few errands.

When we went back to nurse Sam, our plans started to fall off the tracks.

Sam would not wake up to eat. So I gave up and opted to pump and let Sam have a bottle instead. After the feeding, we went to the nearest Christmas tree lot, bought ourselves a beautiful tree, strapped it to the top of the car, and headed home. Along the way we checked in with my parents to see how Irene was doing.

"Well, I don't want to worry you, but she has a pretty high fever," my mom said.

"How else is she feeling?" I asked.

"No clue, she has been asleep for the past two hours."

"OK, when she wakes up, bring her home. We will figure it out."

In the meantime, Peter and I got the tree inside the house, put it in the tree stand, secured it, stood back to admire it, and then watched as the tree toppled over, bending the tree stand. Right at the same time, the phone rang.

"Not a good time, Mom," I said as I picked up the phone.

"Irene woke up covered in vomit and has thrown up three times since then," Mom responded.

"Shit. OK. One of us will be there in a few minutes," I told her.

We divided and conquered: Peter took care of the tree stand, and I headed to my parents' house.

Irene looked terrible and she kept falling asleep mid-sentence. I called the NICU to let them know that I would not be in to feed Sam at 6 p.m. Sam's nurse that evening, Pam, told me to take a big breath, but that Sam had suffered a minor setback. Sometime after we left, Sam had a really bad brady and apnea event. The event was so bad, he did not respond to vigorous stimulation and had to be bagged. Pam assured me that Sam was looking good and acting normal now.

Dr. Sandhu thought the issue was reflux, as the incident happened soon after Sam ate. Reflux is easily treatable, so I took some comfort in his theory. Still, being bagged was nothing to laugh at.

Of course, the event reset the going-home countdown clock back to five days.

A piece of me was relieved knowing that Sam would not be coming home for at least five days. Currently, our house was not safe for Sam. We had a very sick little girl, and every surface of our house was covered with germs. We couldn't take him out of the safety of the NICU into our cesspool of a house.

Chapter 41

Our house was now a cesspool of disease. I woke up the next day with a fever and a sore throat. This meant that I was banned from the NICU—that for the first time in over two months, I would go without seeing Sam for at least one whole day. It would also mean that Sam would spend the entire day without the breast and would have to rely solely on the bottle.

Inside the infirmary, Irene was still vomiting up everything we gave her, and was now on antibiotics, ear drops, and anti-nausea medication. It was the sickest I had ever seen Irene. She just lay in bed with me alternating between sleeping and watching cartoons. I did my best not to worry too much about her, and Sam, and me, but it was hard. I was battling a sore throat and fever and hoping against hope that as shitty as I felt, I would not get any worse.

On top of all of this was the terrible mom guilt that after Sam had such a scary incident the previous night, I had not been able to see him or talk to him. The mom guilt was real.

Despite the previous night's excitement, Sam was moving through his discharge checklist like a champ. First up was the hearing screening. I was not worried about this at all, as Sam had shown over and over that he could hear what was going on around him. He passed his hearing test with flying colors. The next item was to get his first RSV antibody shot, Synagis.

Since Sam entered the NICU, people had talked about two things over and over again with the hushed tones used to talk about cancer: NEC and RSV. I was now an expert on NEC, despite never having to deal with it personally. Now I was starting to learn everything I could about RSV, which presents like a common cold in adults and healthy older children.

"Sam will be going home at one of the more dangerous times for preemies," Teresa told me. "We are deep in cold, flu, and RSV season, and will be until May first."

"Is RSV really that bad?" I asked.

"In preemies and children with weaker lungs or other health issues, RSV can be dangerous, even deadly."

"Great."

"RSV is common and highly contagious," Teresa continued. "One advantage of Sam being so small is he is eligible for the Synagis shot. This will boost his immune system if he is exposed to RSV."

Synagis is expensive, and preemies need more than one dose of it during RSV season. Because of Sam's gestational age and weight at birth, he met the California state standards for five shots of Synagis through the entire season, December to April.

Just having the shots, though, was not going to be enough to protect Sam once he was out of the NICU. Dr. Sandhu told us that for the first five months (or until May 1), we would not be allowed to take Sam into any indoor public locations or any large outdoor crowds. That meant no grocery stores, pharmacies, schools, farmers markets, or restaurants. I would need to get anything and everything I might need delivered.

On Sam's eighty-eighth day in the NICU, he got his first Synagis shot.

He did well with the shot, but later that night he had one brady, and the countdown clock was reset to five days, putting his potential release date at December 19. I could work with December 19.

I had decided that Sam would be home by Christmas, before he reached one hundred days in the NICU.

We were now in full countdown mode. Irene was finally on the mend; my sore throat never developed into anything worse and cleared up after two days.

Dr. Sandhu and Teresa called a meeting to set an official release date for Sam.

"Based on everything I can see, I am comfortable saying that Sam will go home on December twentieth," Dr. Sandhu announced.

"December twentieth," I repeated. "That's what, day ninety-five in the NICU?"

"Yes, I believe that is right."

"Ninety-five. That's a nice round number. And it's before Sam's original due date of January fourth," I said. "But wait, what day of the week is that? There is no way Sam can go home when Laura isn't here."

"Don't worry. I checked before we met, and Laura will be working that day," Teresa assured me.

"Good, because when Sam leaves, Laura is leading the parade."

With a firm release date in hand, relief set in. Holy shit. There was an end to our NICU imprisonment. Freedom was just around the corner.

Just as my smile was taking over, Dr. Sandhu brought me back down to earth.

"All of this is dependent on how Sam does between now and then. Remember, he has to be brady free for five days before we let him go home," Dr. Sandhu reminded me.

And just like that, my relief turned to anxiety. A real end was in sight, but at any moment, that end could be pushed further and further away.

I started thinking about the mother I met my third week in the NICU who was on the countdown to take her baby home. Every time she would get to day four of the five-day countdown, her little girl would have a brady. I saw the devastation and frustration on her face. The fourth time this happened, I watched this woman break, as the push and pull finally overwhelmed her. At the time I felt bad for her; now I was starting to understand how she'd felt.

The first day after we set Sam's release date came and went without any excitement. He nursed, he slept, and he pooped. The next day, more of the same. Two days down, three days to go.

Part of the discharge process is a car seat test. This is a simple test in which Sam had to sit strapped into his infant car seat for an hour and be monitored to make sure his oxygen levels didn't dip. He passed with flying colors.

Now the only obstacle between us and bringing Sam home was a potential brady. I became obsessed with Sam's monitors again. From the moment I arrived at the NICU to the moment I left, I stared at the monitors. I was convinced that if I stared at them long and hard enough, there was no way they would dare cross me and dip, thereby resetting our release date by five days. When I wasn't at the hospital, I visualized the monitors. Anytime the phone rang, my heart would jump into my throat, convinced it would be the hospital calling to say Sam had had a brady.

Then it happened.

On day three of the five-day countdown, Sam had a brady. He had just finished nursing, and I was putting him back in his crib when the alarm bells sounded. He corrected right away, and for a fleeting moment, since his nurse had stepped out of the room, I thought about not telling anyone. Other than Sam, I was the only one who knew it had happened. I toyed with keeping this secret, until I realized that I would never forgive myself if I didn't tell someone and they let him go home before he was ready. I called Teresa over and told her what happened.

"Teresa, Sam had a small brady."

"Shit . . . Tell me everything. What happened right before the brady, how bad was it, how was his recovery?"

I took a deep breath. "He had just nursed for a long time, and I was putting him back in his crib. It happened really quickly. The moment the alarms went off, he self-corrected."

"How low did his heart rate go?"

"I don't know. Low enough to set off the alarms."

"It was right after he ate?"

"Yes."

"Was he lying flat?"

"Yes."

By now, tears were starting to well up as the reality that Sam would not be going home on the twentieth was setting in.

"OK."

Teresa looked at me then looked at Sam.

"I don't think this one counts. I am blaming reflux."

And like that, my hope was restored. Teresa was not resetting the countdown clock. Sam was still on track to go home.

Chapter 42

S hit. Sam was still on track to go home.

After ninety-plus days, we should be more than ready for Sam to come home, right?

Wrong. Our house was in dire need of a deep cleaning. We needed a crew to come and clean every surface. We had to rewash all of the bassinet linens to remove the thick layer of cat hair our three cats had deposited by sleeping in it for months. For that matter, we needed to train the damn cats that the bassinet was not a bed for them anymore.

Aside from the housework, there was all the mental preparation. I would no longer have nurses and doctors at my side. The apnea and brady monitor that I had become so attached to was not coming home with us. I would have to rely on my instinct as Sam's mom.

I was plagued with doubt and questions. What if Sam desaturated or had a brady in his sleep? What if I was asleep when this happened and I didn't know? What if he didn't self-correct? Honestly, I was starting to think being in the NICU wasn't such a bad idea. I needed that monitor. I needed those alarms. I needed Laura and Teresa to be right there by my side. I could not do this without them—could I?

I had to have a talk with Sam. If I was really going to bring him home in two days, without any medical monitoring or nurses, he had to understand that breathing was part of the deal.

"Kiddo. Listen. In two days, you are coming home. I need you to do one thing for me—breathe. Never forget to breathe. Can you do that for me?" I asked while kissing him on the cheek.

Chapter 43

After ninety-five days as NICU parents, we had finally arrived at graduation day. Knowing that we were going to be pretty much housebound until the end of RSV season, all of us, my parents included, headed out for breakfast.

Truth be told, I was not in a hurry to leave the NICU. I was still terrified by the idea of bringing Sam home, so the longer we took to get to the hospital, the longer it would be before the responsibility for Sam was all on me. We took our time eating, relishing the morning, enjoying the molasses pancakes, and savoring our last few moments of freedom not consumed by the responsibility of caring for a former micro-preemie.

"I think it's time we wrapped this up," my dad said.

"Just a few more minutes," I pleaded.

"Honey. You are ready. Go get your boy and bring him home," my mom said, smiling at me.

We had stalled long enough. My parents had planned a big, fun day for Irene. They wanted to make sure she was occupied and distracted.

Irene was a bit on edge that morning. Perhaps the anticipation of her brother coming home and all that came with it was more than her five-year-old brain could process. She alternated between being sweet and excited, from telling us to thank all the doctors and nurses for letting Sam go home, to downright crabby. I hoped that spending the day with my parents at the zoo was what Irene needed.

We arrived at the hospital like conquering warriors returning from battle. We had been at war, fighting for our son's survival since I first arrived in Labor & Delivery. Now our fears melted away. We were finally leaving the hospital with our son. We were entering those doors for the last time.

When we walked into the NICU, Allison and Sonia at the front desk were all smiles.

"Graduation day!" they called out when they saw us in the hallway.

Seeing how excited they were got me more excited.

As we walked through the NICU, every nurse, orderly, technician, doctor, and staff member we passed was smiling at us. The word was out that Sam was going home.

This time, walking back to Sam's room, I didn't feel like I was checking another day off the calendar. Each person we saw congratulated us and told us how excited they were for us and how much they would miss Sam.

We got to Sam's room and just sat, each of us in a glider rocker.

We were leaving.

It was over.

Sam was free to go.

But we didn't leave just yet. In fact, I think we hung out for over three hours, talking with people. We were savoring the moment—but I was also dragging my feet just a little. The NICU had become my home, and the people who worked there were my family and support system.

Finally, as her shift was coming to an end, Laura decided to take charge.

"Melissa, let's do this."

"I'm not ready. Not yet."

"Bullshit. You're ready. Sam wants out of here. Look at him. It's time."

"Five more minutes?"

"Nope. Now."

And just like that, Laura turned off the monitor, removed the leads from Sam, swaddled him, and smiled at me.

As Laura was picking Sam up out of his crib, Misty came in with a special baby mortarboard for Sam to wear for his graduation.

His outfit complete, Laura, Sam, Misty, Peter, and I began the walk out the door—Laura leading the way with Sam safely tucked in her arms, Peter and I trailing just slightly behind her.

Everyone we passed stopped to give us a hug. It must have taken us fifteen minutes to go from the back of the NICU to the front desk. When we finally made it to the front, Sonia had the honor of cutting off our blue hospital wristbands. This simple act was the last symbolic gesture freeing us from our NICU prison.

From there, it was just the four of us: Peter, Laura, Sam, and me. We paused at the security desk to introduce one of our favorite guards to Sam. In the elevator ride down, I started to cry.

We had done it.

Laura saw my tears and, firmly but sweetly, said, "Get it together, girl. Last thing you get to do is make me cry."

When we got to the lobby, Laura decided that the moment wasn't right without music, so she hummed the graduation march.

As we walked through the doors of the hospital, Sam got his first whiff of fresh air and the sun touched his skin, unobstructed, for the first time. Bathed in that sunlight, Sam looked like just any other normal newborn, heading home to start his new life.

Part Three

The First Year
at Home

Chapter 44

Once Sam was safely tucked into his car seat, I climbed into the back seat and exhaled. Peter turned to look at me from the driver's seat and with the largest smile I had ever seen on his face said, "We did it. Let's go home!"

I had made a special playlist for the drive home. I'd had ninety-five days to think about what songs I wanted Sam to hear as we drove the seven miles from Alta Bates to our house. The first was Jimmy Cliff singing "I Can See Clearly Now." Peter cranked the volume up as he pulled out of the hospital patient loading area. As momentous as this occasion was, Sam didn't have a clue. Sometime between my hugs and my sobs on Laura's shoulder as we said our goodbyes, Sam had fallen sound asleep in his car seat.

Even though Sam was asleep, I held his little hand and told him about everything we were driving by. I wanted him to know about the big, wonderful world outside the hospital walls. I talked to him about trees, parks, bikes, cafés, school, our house, and everything else that popped into my head.

I had a lot of time to talk, as Peter drove about ten miles per hour the whole way home. He was not going to take any chances that a bump in the road would startle Sam and cause him to have an apnea or a brady and send us right back to the NICU.

When we got home, my parents' car was in front of our house.

As we made our way to the front door, I could hear Irene singing inside. The moment she heard the key in the lock, her singing turned to screams of joy. I could not make out what she was screaming, but I had to assume it was something like "SAM IS HERE!"

The minute we walked inside, Irene came rushing toward us. Preemie mom instinct kicked in, and I grabbed Irene before she could put her hands on Sam and demanded she use the hand sanitizer that was located all over our house. This would be the start of a new ritual for anyone who came into our home.

Sanitize first, say hello second.

With her hands now clean, Irene leaned into the car seat and kissed Sam on every possible surface she could get her lips on. I finally had to pull Irene off her brother.

"Kiddo, take a breath. Sam is home. You will be able to kiss him anytime you want," I reminded her.

"I want to kiss him more now," she demanded.

"How about you let me get him to the living room, and then you can get back to kissing him, OK?"

"Fine," she said, running down the stairs to ensure prime kissing position.

All of us, my parents included, spent the next few hours staring at Sam and exclaiming that we couldn't believe he was home. My parents finally broke free. It was dinnertime, and they felt it was important for Sam's first dinner at home to be just the four of us.

They were right.

We had been a four-person family for ninety-five days, but this was the first time we were all together, just us at the family dinner table. Every little thing that happened that night felt so special. And honestly, nothing really even happened. It was just everyday normal life—something none of us had experienced since I was admitted to the hospital 101 days earlier.

That humdrum normalcy was fantastic.

Imagine, for Sam, this family meal was the first time in his life he had ever been around food. For all of my NICU meals, I'd had to leave Sam's room and either go to the cafeteria or the family room to eat. Now laid out on the table was a Chinese feast my parents had brought in and all the wonderful smells associated with it.

For me, the basic concept of eating AND holding Sam had been just a pipe dream. Now I was living that dream. It was the first of many normal life firsts that I would experience.

Of course, as had happened many times in the NICU, my enjoyment of normal life was cut short by the cry of the electronic baby. Despite being a good eater, Sam still required one to two bottles of breast milk twice a day, as he was still taking vitamins and iron, and had to have some breast milk fortified with high-calorie formula. That meant, aside from nursing, I would still be attached to the electronic baby for a little bit longer.

I really didn't care. Sam was home. Everything else was unimportant.

Chapter 45

The euphoria of Sam being home dulled a little when he would not sleep or, as he had now discovered the power of crying, would not stop wailing unless he was held. It was a long first few nights at home—made worse by the fact that the flu both Irene and I had was now working its way through Peter.

By mid-afternoon on Sam's first full day at home, Peter was in such bad shape, I had to send him to my parents' house for sleep and quarantine. That meant I was on my own with both kids.

At least we had an activity to do: visit Sam's pediatrician for a checkup and weigh-in.

I was nervous about taking Sam to the doctor during the height of flu and RSV season. After all, doctors' offices are usually filled with sick people. Luckily, Teresa had told us to tell the receptionist that Sam was a preemie and needed to be taken back to a room right away.

Before the receptionist could even say hello, I spoke up.

"Hi. We need to be taken to a room right away. This is Sam, he was—" I was cut off before I could finish.

"Melissa!" a voice called out from the other side of the reception desk. "Come back. Come back."

It was Dr. Sarah, Sam's pediatrician.

Dr. Sarah was delighted to see Sam outside of the NICU. She

had been following his progress since he was born, even visiting him once a week. Now she was seeing him in the quiet of her own office. She gave Sam a quick once-over and beamed.

"My God, he looks so good!" Dr. Sarah exclaimed. "Yesterday was so much fun," she added.

"Why is that?" I asked.

"I got to erase Sam's name from our hospital board."

"Your hospital board?"

"Yep—we keep a list of names of all of our patients who are hospitalized. Sam had been up there the longest. I *loved* erasing his name!"

I believed her. She looked so pleased that Sam was free.

The rest of the visit was quick and painless. The biggest thing we learned at this visit was Sam's weight: he now clocked in at a whopping five pounds, seven ounces. I couldn't help but smile. I loved hearing Sam's weight now that he was finally the size of many full-term newborns.

The kids and I spent a quiet afternoon playing board games and hanging out.

It was perfect. I was home. I had both of my children with me. They were both healthy. What more could I want?

For the first time in months, I felt like I could breathe again.

Chapter 46

Of course, this idyllic family portrait only lasted a day. After the rush of Sam's arrival home wore off, our new expanded family became harder for Irene to accept. I was tied to either a pump or Sam. Plus, with it being RSV season, there were very few places we could all go as a family.

Peter was back from his quarantine at my parents' house, and Irene wanted to go out for breakfast.

"You and Dad can go, but Sam and I would have to stay here."

"But, Mom. I want you and Sam there too," Irene whined loudly.

"I know, kiddo. But it's not safe for Sam, and I have his food supply with me."

"Fine. Can we go to the movies?"

"Again, you and Dad can go, but Sam and I would have to stay here."

This went on for a while. I had to remind her that Sam was on "house arrest" until the end of RSV season, and since I was pumping and nursing, I was restricted on how long I could be away.

All of this made things harder on Irene. She started acting out, first by talking back, and soon after by throwing huge temper tantrums. It didn't help that she was on winter break from kindergarten and isolated from all of her friends.

I knew we just needed to get to Christmas, and the chaos that was a five-year-old on Christmas morning would make everything better. Besides, my brother was arriving from Africa on Christmas morning—something Irene knew nothing about. I just had to make it to Tío's arrival, and everything would be OK.

By the time Christmas finally rolled around, Irene had become a terror. She wouldn't eat anything I cooked. She refused to go to bed at bedtime. She yelled at me constantly. She argued with her dad about everything possible. It was understandable, but that didn't make it better. On Christmas morning, as we gathered around the tree, I wasn't sure Irene was going to be able to wait for my parents and her big surprise to arrive.

Luckily, the doorbell rang early, and when Irene opened the door to see my brother, her beloved tío, standing there, her entire mood changed. She leapt onto my brother and clung there until we finally asked her to at least let him come in. After that, everything was bliss.

I have no idea what gifts were given or received. All I can remember is sitting on the floor of my living room with Sam laid across my lap, Irene curled on the couch next to my brother, my parents sitting next to each other, and Peter taking as many pictures as the memory card could handle. It was everything I wanted. For a moment, everything was good.

Chapter 47

My plan to have a second child had become a reality. Now I could enjoy all that I had and focus on keeping Sam healthy.

Growing was not a problem for Sam. Dr. Sarah told us that she wanted to see Sam gain a half an ounce every day. The way he was eating, I was not worried. In just one week, Sam had met and surpassed his goal, gaining between one to two ounces a day.

"Since he is doing such a great job, do you think we can stop the fortified bottles? They seem to give Sam gas and constipate him," I asked.

"We can try. Let's stop for three days and then have you guys come back for a weigh-in. If there is no impact on his weight gain, then we will agree to stop all the fortified milk," Dr. Sarah agreed.

When Sam's next appointment rolled around, Irene insisted on coming with us as opposed to staying with my parents. I think she just wanted to be a part of whatever it was we were doing. The four of us piled into the car and headed to the pediatrician.

Once again, the moment we arrived we asked to be put in a room. This time we didn't have to ask twice, as apparently a note on Sam's file said to take us to isolation on arrival for all future appointments. I guess you could call that a perk of being a preemie.

We waited in that room for a long time. There were a lot of sick kids in the office that day. The nurse told us that Dr. Sarah was about thirty minutes or more behind schedule.

Irene was restless. She sat on my lap, then Peter's, then the exam table, then back to me. A doctor's office is hard enough when you are the patient, but even worse when you are the sister of the patient. Tired of Irene's constant demands for attention, I handed her *Hop on Pop* and told her to look at the pictures.

Irene picked up the book, opened to the first page, and said, "Up pup. Pup is up."

Peter and I turned toward Irene. She had never so much as tried to sound words out before, so we were totally taken aback.

Irene turned the page. "Cup Pup. Pup in cup," she continued.

Peter put his hand on her arm. We didn't want to say anything, in case the spell might be broken.

When Irene had finished *Hop on Pop*, Peter and I didn't say anything. We were waiting to see what would happen next. Finally, Peter broke the tension.

"Irene. Did you just read your brother a book?"

"Yep!"

"When did you learn how to do that?"

"What do you mean, Daddy? I could always do that!"

Irene had no idea what she had done, but that didn't stop us from showering her with praise and kisses.

Dr. Sarah came in just then. "What's all the commotion?" she asked, smiling.

Irene beamed and said, "I read Sam a book."

The looks on our faces said it all, because Dr. Sarah

disappeared and came back with a special princess ring for Irene to celebrate her achievement.

In all the excitement, I had almost forgotten why we were at the pediatrician in the first place.

"Well, Melissa, let's get Sam on a scale and see what the last three days have done for him," Dr. Sarah said.

I stripped Sam down and placed him on the scale. I held my breath.

"Well?" I asked tentatively.

"I hope you brought the preemie formula with you, because you can return it to the NICU," Dr. Sarah said, beaming.

"Really? What was the weight gain?" I asked.

"He gained five ounces since you were last here. That's more than his previous pattern."

"Hell yeah!" I yelled, high-fiving Peter for good measure.

We left Dr. Sarah's on a high. Irene was now officially a reader, and Sam was one step closer to being a typical newborn—well, as typical as an almost-four-month-old newborn can be.

When the clock struck midnight on New Year's Eve, I did my best to close the chapter on my years and years of fertility struggles and the long NICU haul. The close of 2010 became symbolic of much more than just the end of a year—it was the end of a struggle. For obvious reasons, it had not been my favorite year. Yes, my son was born in 2010, but trust me, I would much rather have been in my last weeks of pregnancy complaining about my swollen ankles and heartburn than nursing my son into the New Year.

I was grateful that Sam was alive, home, and thriving, but the trauma of the previous year hung in the air. While I sat in the glider rocker in my bedroom nursing Sam in the middle of the night, I made a resolution to let all the stress and tension of the previous year go and to celebrate all the good we had going for us.

Yeah, right!

Did I really think it would be that easy to just let it all go? After all that we had been through and all that was still ahead of us?

At least I would keep my tradition of making New Year's resolutions I had no intention of keeping.

Chapter 48

Once Irene got over the disruption of her brother's homecoming, she was clearly the one person adjusting the best to our new family. She loved having her brother home. More than that, she loved being a big sister and was eager to help. If we needed a bottle warmed, Irene was there to volunteer. If Sam dropped his blue lovey, Irene would swoop in to pick it up before we even knew it was on the floor.

She drew the line at diapers. She wanted to help, but she wasn't a saint. She thought diapers were disgusting. Who could blame her? And Sam did go through a lot of them in a day.

Since it was the winter break for Irene, the house was filled with people and activity. Peter had another week off work and took a week of vacation time. Irene had at least another week off from school. My brother was staying until the second week of January before returning to Lesotho. Best of all, my grandfather came up from Los Angeles for a visit.

Seeing my grandfather hold his great-grandson (and namesake) for the first time was heartwarming.

When we told him that we had given Sam his name, he laughed and told us it wasn't possible. He was adamant that Sam was named after my uncle and not him. I tried to reason with him and tell him that Sam was named for both of them.

"No, he's not, Melissa."

"Why not, Papa?"

"He's named for your uncle."

"I think I would know who I named my son after," I teased.

"You can't name someone after someone who is alive." (This is a Jewish tradition I was not aware of.)

"Well, I guess I am not following that rule, then!"

Somewhat resigned, my grandfather smiled and let it go.

Throughout this entire exchange, Sam had been contributing with those cute cooing noises babies make.

"So, Papa. Since Sam is awake, would you like to hold him?" I asked, already on my feet moving toward my grandfather.

He laughed. "No, no. I'm fine looking at him."

"Come on. It's your great-grandson," I prodded. "Your namesake," I added for good measure.

Papa chuckled. Before he could say no a second time, I quickly placed Sam in my grandfather's arms. Peter was ready with the camera. He snapped about three pictures before my grandfather smiled and said, "OK, OK. Now take the baby back." Papa was never very comfortable holding a baby, but there was no way I was not going to have a picture of them together.

By the time my grandfather headed back to Los Angeles and my brother returned to Lesotho, it was time for Irene to go back to school, and for our life to settle into its new routine.

Chapter 49

As much as I love a good plan, I love a good family routine even more. Before Sam, the routine was easy. On weekdays, I got up first, showered, and got dressed. Then, while Peter was getting ready, I would wake Irene up, help her get dressed for school, make a quick breakfast, and while she ate, make her lunch. Peter drove her to school and headed to work while I took the train to my job in San Francisco. In the afternoon, I picked up Irene from school, and the two of us had almost two hours together to make dinner and hang out before Peter got home from work. Once we all ate a nice family dinner, Irene would get a bath, and Peter would read her to sleep while I got some downtime.

That all seemed so simple and idyllic now.

With Sam, the routine became a chaotic mess of making it work and hoping we didn't forget something.

It was clear to us in the first few weeks that there was no way Sam would sleep anywhere that wasn't attached to me. We had set up a bassinet in our room next to our bed. Even though I could drape my arm into the bassinet, Sam was having none of it. If he was dead asleep and I tried to lay him in the bassinet, he would wake up and start crying. The only way to get Sam to sleep was next to me in our bed.

I know. Most medical experts frown upon co-sleeping.

I know. We were warned excessively at discharge not to co-sleep with Sam, as the suffocation danger is too much of a risk.

Whatever.

I needed sleep, and the only way I was going to get that was to let Sam sleep in our bed.

That, of course, made our new routine really interesting.

Because I was up most of the night either nursing Sam, pumping, or waking up in a panic that I had smothered Sam in my sleep, Peter now had to get up first and help Irene get ready for school. As soon as she was almost ready to leave, Peter let Irene loose into our room to wake me up and cover me with kisses. Well, really, she wanted to cover Sam with kisses, but she had to get past me to do that.

Once everyone was properly kissed, Peter took Irene to school before heading off to work. I was still out on disability, so my day consisted of taking care of Sam. Because we were still deep in the throes of RSV season, Sam and I were limited in what we could do during the day. Unlike most new moms, I could not join a mommy group or spend my mornings wandering the aisles of Target. If I needed diapers or aspirin or just about anything, I had to go shopping in the evening when Peter was home or turn to the Internet. I spent a lot of time on the Internet and was on a first-name basis with our UPS delivery man, Doug.

Once it was time to pick up Irene, Sam and I headed out for our one excursion of the day. Irene was in an after-school program at her elementary school until 5 p.m. To avoid taking Sam into the petri dish known as her classroom, I worked out an arrangement with the head of the program that she would bring Irene to the gate of the school every day at 5:15. This allowed me to keep Sam safely in the car, protected from any of the possible germs.

As soon as Irene, Sam, and I got home, I made dinner (or, in most instances, I ordered it from a local restaurant) and we hung out. This wasn't the same as it used to be for Irene, as my attention was more divided. Sam required a lot of my time, something that Irene understood. Occasionally.

By the time Peter got home, I was exhausted after all day with a needy baby. I looked forward to the moment both kids were asleep so I could collapse in bed with the TV playing something mindless in the background. Of course, Sam was usually asleep on my chest or attached to my breast, so there wasn't much room to collapse.

My isolation from the adult world was overwhelming. Before I had Sam, I had a job in San Francisco with people I really liked. Every day, I would get to dress up, ride BART to the city, and work with interesting people, many of whom were friends. On weekends, we met friends for brunch, took Irene to classes, visited one of the many local parks, hung out with friends, and generally acted like real people who were part of the world.

Once I had Sam, all of that went away. At first, isolation wasn't a problem, as I was welcomed into a new social world in the NICU filled with kind nurses, doctors, social workers, hospital employees, and fellow preemie parents. Each day I had lots of people to talk to and visit with.

I was still part of something.

Now, however, my social world had been reduced to Peter, Irene, Sam, my parents, and daily pleasantries with Doug from UPS.

Oh, and visits from Sam's home health-care workers.

Due to Sam's birth weight, we had qualified for a number of state services. My favorites were his Special Start nurse and his Regional Center of the East Bay evaluations. Each of these services brought wonderful people to my house either weekly or monthly.

Sam's nurse, Marguerite, came weekly. She was a warm and reassuring presence in my life. Marguerite brought a scale so I could weigh Sam weekly and track his impressive weight gain. She was also there to answer any questions I had and, most importantly, to talk me off whatever ledge I managed to walk myself out on.

"Sam's diapers are dry every morning."

"OK."

"Not a drop of pee. Like when his kidneys stopped working in the NICU. Dry as a bone."

"Does he have wet diapers during the day?"

"Of course. Lots of them. But not at night. I don't think his kidneys work at night."

"Or . . . he just doesn't pee at night right now. It could just be that."

"You sure his kidneys are working?"

"Well, he just peed on my scale, so I think they are working."

That was a pretty typical exchange between the two of us: me building up to a crisis and Marguerite calmly bringing me back down.

The folks from the regional center came to evaluate Sam's developmental progress. It was always reassuring to have their evaluation following an evaluation at the pediatrician's office, which was based on Sam's actual age. Corrected age is based on what age he would have been had he been born on his due date. Most medical professionals correct a preemie's age until they are two, when they are magically supposed to have caught up.

At the appointment with the pediatrician, Sam would do quite poorly in his evaluation. Then the regional center would come by, do the same evaluation against his corrected age, and he would fare much better. That was great because I needed to be talked off a panic ledge, and the regional center team always obliged.

Notice a theme there—Melissa in a panic . . . calm and supportive professionals stepping in to talk me down?

⁓

The idea of actual age versus corrected age was one I struggled to keep straight. It felt like I was shortchanging Sam if I told people his corrected age, but there were days when I couldn't take the strange looks and off-putting comments when I gave Sam's actual age. Imagine seeing a little six-pound newborn and being told he is almost four months old. Or imagine meeting a little six-pound newborn who could hold his head up without help. No matter what answer I gave to the simple question of "How old is your baby?" I was always met with a look of confusion.

Things were even more complicated before Sam's due date—or, as my brother coined it, Sam's re-birth day. His corrected age was in gestational weeks—so that really threw people.

On Sam's due date, I went to a hospital-sponsored developmental playgroup for NICU grads. It was refreshing to be out amongst other people, adults and preemie parents. We all went around the room introducing our babies and ourselves. Everyone was giving his or her baby's actual and corrected age. Then it was my turn.

"Hi. I am Melissa and this is Sam."

(Room mumbles, "Hi.")

"Sam is four months actual . . . and well. Um, what is the date today?"

"January fourth," someone replied.

"Oh. Wow. So I guess that Sam's corrected age is zero. Today is his due date."

The look on everyone's face was priceless. Had I been with non-preemie parents, I don't think the reaction would have been nearly as heartwarming. These were all parents who got it. They knew in their bones how amazing it was for Sam to be alive.

⁓

As Sam got older, the question of age became even harder to answer. I found myself stuttering and stumbling when strangers would ask me how old my baby was. Sometimes I was doing the math in my head between corrected and actual age. Sometimes I was assessing whether I wanted to share the story of Sam's birth with a total stranger. Sometimes I was so confused with the entire question that my mind just went blank. No matter what, I always felt like my answer was not good enough.

If I gave his actual age, the most common response was "He is so small!" That would just rile me up. I wanted to shake the person and scream, "Are you freaking kidding me?"

If I gave his corrected age, I felt like I was cheating Sam out of four months of his life and his struggle. But at least I was spared a long, sometimes uncomfortable conversation.

There were days when I would give his actual age followed by his corrected age. It was the most honest but often led to a long conversation. Sometimes the person would just look horrified and say, "Oh." Other times they would tell me that their brother/sister/neighbor/friend/coworker also had a preemie. More often than not, I would see that look of shock and awe that he was so early and now so big.

It was a simple question that I dreaded being asked. Such a simple inquiry with such a loaded answer.

Chapter 50

At home, we'd finally gotten into a rhythm. Of course, that was a rhythm colored by sleep deprivation. Now that Sam was no longer in the hospital, the angst and anxiety of having a baby in the NICU was replaced with the normal sleep deprivation of having a newborn baby. As the sleepless nights added up, we began functioning like normal parents of a newborn: acting like complete and total zombies.

We found ourselves forgetting the simplest of tasks, trailing off mid-thought while in a conversation, and falling asleep at the most inopportune times. It was during this time that we did the one thing people joke about but often never admit to doing . . . we broke the baby.

Well, technically, Peter broke the baby.

"Broke" is a bit of a harsh description, but "dropped the baby on its head" doesn't sound all that much better.

It was late at night, and Sam had woken up screaming and hungry. Peter volunteered to take this one on, and I was not inclined to argue with him. I needed to sleep.

As Peter tells it, he fell asleep on the guest bed with Sam asleep on his chest. He thinks he moved in his sleep, and as luck would have it, Sam made a move at the exact same time. Dad went one way and Sam went another. Sadly, the direction Sam went was off

Daddy's chest, off the mattress, onto the bed frame made of rebar and wrapped in straw, and then down to the hardwood floor.

Sam's screams woke me up immediately. They were loud. Louder than I had ever heard before.

As I ran into the room, the look on Peter's face said it all—something terrible had happened.

"What is going on?"

"I . . . I . . . I dropped him."

"What do you mean, you dropped him?" I asked, trying to assess the situation.

"Oh God. I dropped him on his head. Oh God. Oh God."

Peter was sobbing uncontrollably now.

"Look at me. Tell me what happened. You have to tell me what happened." I was trying to stay calm so one of us could figure out what to do next.

While Peter sobbed, Sam was wailing in his arms. I finally picked Sam up and brought him to our room to nurse. I figured putting a boob in his mouth would either calm him down or make things worse. Luckily, Sam latched on and began sucking down milk.

Peter followed me back to our room and told me what happened.

"Did he ever lose consciousness?" I asked. I knew this was important.

"I don't think so. He screamed the minute he hit the bed."

"So—he was crying the whole time?"

"Yes."

"Well, he is nursing well right now and calm. Let's call the on-call doctor and see what she says."

We got a call back within ten minutes. Peter told them what happened. Because Sam hadn't lost consciousness, the doctor was not overly concerned. She told us if his condition changed, to take him to the ER right away. We also made an appointment to see Sam's pediatrician first thing Monday morning.

Since this event happened on a Saturday night, the only way he could be seen by a doctor was to go to the hospital. Being RSV season, the hospital was the most dangerous place for a preemie like Sam.

I stayed up all night rocking and nursing Sam. I did not put that boy down for anything. He came with me to the bathroom. He came with me when I needed a snack. I was not going to let him out of my sight until I knew he was OK. I really wanted a doctor to look at him, but the thought of the ER on a Saturday night in RSV season was just too scary.

Luckily, Marguerite called us early the next morning to see if she could come by for a visit. I wept as I told her to come now—and explained what had happened.

She was at our house within the hour. She stayed with us for a few hours, monitoring Sam and keeping me calm.

"He is eating well, and from what I can see, his behavior is normal," Marguerite said reassuringly.

"Do you see the puffiness on his head, though?" I asked.

"I do. It doesn't look too bad, but we will just keep watching it. I have a measuring tape with me; let's measure his head and recheck in an hour."

I liked this idea. It gave me a metric to focus on.

Irene was at a playdate, so she was blissfully unaware of what was going on.

By the time Marguerite left, we were feeling a little better about things. Sam had eaten well all day and was not overly fussy or overly calm, and the swelling hadn't increased all day. We agreed that if anything changed or if we started to get nervous again, we would take Sam to the ER.

~

That night I continued my vigil, holding Sam and not getting a wink of sleep. I was going on forty-eight hours of no sleep, but I didn't care. I had to make sure Sam was OK. Peter fared better, got a good night sleep, seemed to have let go of his concerns, and headed to work.

On Monday morning, Sam and I went to see Dr. Sarah. I filled her in on the past two days. Dr. Sarah listened intently and then began to examine Sam's head.

"What are your plans for the rest of the day, Melissa?" she asked, sounding more concerned than I would have liked.

"I was going to leave Sam with my parents and chaperone Irene's class Valentine's party."

Dr. Sarah, who always has an air of calm about her, wrinkled her face a little and asked me bluntly, "Can someone else do that?"

"I am sure I could find someone, but it means so much to Irene to have me there."

"Well, I really need you to find someone else to cover for you."

"It would just be for an hour," I argued, still not fully aware of what was going on.

"Melissa, you need to take Sam to the ER." To ensure her point was being heard, she added a very stern "Now."

My heart started to race and my hands began to shake.

"I don't like the way Sam's skull looks and feels. I am concerned he has a skull fracture."

I stared blankly at her.

"Melissa, I am going to call the ER at Children's Hospital so they know you are coming, but you and Sam need to go there. Now."

I nodded, stood up, and began to cry.

"I . . . I can't move," I sobbed.

Dr. Sarah came over to me. "I know this is terrifying, but you can do this."

After a few minutes of sitting with Dr. Sarah, I pulled it together enough to drive the short distance from her office to Children's Hospital, calling my parents and Peter along the way.

When I arrived at Children's Hospital, the triage people knew who Sam and I were and took us back to an isolation room right away.

It took about an hour and a half for Peter to get from his job in San Francisco to the hospital. He looked shaken when he arrived and had trouble making eye contact with me. He felt guilty, and I was too tired and worried to comfort him.

We sat around the ER for about four hours doing nothing but staring at the hidden object poster on the wall. Finally, we were taken upstairs for a CT scan. While we waited for the results, a social worker came to interview us about what had happened.

A baby with a head injury sets off warning bells at social services, which meant Peter and I needed to be cleared as fit parents. The conversation was very uncomfortable. Peter adjusted his position in his chair a lot. My hold on Sam became a bit more possessive. The interview was well into its thirtieth minute when a resident entered the room.

"Do you feel your child is safe alone with your husband?" the social worker asked bluntly.

"Excuse me," the resident interrupted. "I know these parents. I met them at the Alta Bates NICU. These are very attentive parents. I have utter confidence that Sam is safe with both of them."

This vote of confidence satisfied the social worker, and she left.

"I know that was uncomfortable, but we have to be sure," the resident said to us, trying to be reassuring. "I remember you and Sam from my NICU rotation. Wish we were seeing each other under different circumstances."

"Thank you for defending us," I said.

"Of course."

At this point, we were joined by the main ER doctor, who had the CT results.

"Your son has three skull fractures," he started. "The good news is they are the good kind of skull fractures."

Peter was crying in a corner. I moved in closer to the doctor so I could understand better what he meant by "good skull fractures."

"There are two kinds—one where the fracture causes the skull bones to push down into the brain, and the other where the pieces along the fracture move like a fault line. Sam has the second kind."

We were told to go home and monitor Sam closely. If there was any change in his behavior, we were supposed to bring him right back.

We headed home and tried to relax. I was sleep-deprived and still not convinced that everything with Sam was OK. Peter was a guilty mess. On top of all of that, we had done nothing to prepare our house for the coming visit of my in-laws, who live in Dallas, their first since Sam was born.

Peter took the night shift that night, sitting next to Sam's crib and letting me sleep. But every little sound woke me up immediately, as I was sure it was Sam gasping for air or worse. This went on for two more nights. I had surpassed the zombie phase of sleep deprivation and was now just a shell. By the fourth night, I was useless, Peter remained on edge, and Irene was wound up with excitement over her grandparents' visit in two days.

Sam, who had been doing really well since the ER visit, suddenly became very irritable. Then he began to scream. When that wasn't enough, he began channeling Linda Blair in *The Exorcist* and projectile vomited all over his room.

Then the power in our house went out.

I panicked.

Everything the ER and Sam's doctor told us to look for was happening all at once: personality change, inability to be comforted, and vomiting.

The lack of power was just a bonus.

We called the emergency number of the pediatrician's office and waited patiently for a call back. In the ten minutes it took the doctor to call back, I had already packed a bag for the hospital and was ready to go.

"This is Dr. Vo. I have seen the notes from your visit with Dr. Sarah and the ER. Tell me what is going on."

"In the past twenty minutes, Sam has been very irritable and has been projectile vomiting."

"Stop there. Take him back to Children's right away. I will call them. He needs to be checked again."

My instincts were right.

Peter would stay home with Irene. Sam and I would go alone.

Sam and I spent four hours in the ER before they decided to admit us for observation. The ER was not very busy that night. The rooms around us were empty, which made things quiet—eerily quiet. Sam had finally exhausted himself enough that he fell asleep, so the only real sounds I had to focus on were his breathing. I spent the next four hours counting how many breaths Sam took every minute. It was right in the normal range of ninety breaths per minute. This had no real bearing on how his brain was doing, but it just made me feel better.

As we entered our fifth hour in the ER, social services had to come and talk to me again, just to make sure I felt safe with my husband. This was the last thing I had the patience for.

"Can you tell me how this happened?"

"I already told the social worker the last time we were here. My husband fell asleep holding the baby," I snapped back at her.

"The extent of the injuries is not consistent with a simple fall."

Before she could say anything else, I interrupted her. "He hit the bed frame first, which is made of rebar, then hit the uncarpeted floor. It. Was. An. Accident." I punctuated the last line for emphasis.

"I have to ask this, but do you feel safe with your husband in the home?"

"Look, I know you are just doing your job, but please . . . stop. He fell asleep. Was it stupid? Yes. Was it careless? Yes. Could it have been prevented? I don't know. He is a dad of a newborn. He was tired. It was an accident."

I think I said the last part more to remind myself that it wasn't Peter's fault, per se. It could have happened to anyone.

Because it was RSV season, Sam and I were put in an isolation room in the hospital ward. Sam had a cage-like crib, and I had a small padded chair that could supposedly fold out into a lumpy bed. From my chair, I could see bed after bed of very sick babies and their worried parents. Had Sam not been a preemie, we would not have been in the isolation room but out on the ward, which just looked awful.

In the end, Sam and I spent thirty-six hours under observation at the hospital. Sam's personality returned to normal almost as soon as we were admitted, but I am sure they kept us more for my benefit than for Sam's.

"We are concerned with your ability to care for Sam if you don't allow yourself to sleep," the doctor assigned to Sam told me.

"I can't close my eyes. I need to watch him."

"Not here. We are here for that. He is being monitored, so you can relax. You are not alone."

It was a nice thought, at least.

Sam passed all his neurological tests and was discharged with a case of severe reflux that happened to present itself right at the same time as he was dropped on his head.

I left the hospital exhausted, relieved, and with orders to visit a pediatric gastroenterologist for treatment for the reflux.

Only in my family would you get three skull fractures and end up with a gastroenterology referral!

Chapter 51

Since our ER stay, Sam began having more incidents of scream-ing and vomiting. These incidents were coupled with severe constipation.

It was not a pretty combination.

After a number of tests looking at every part of Sam's digestive tract, the pediatric gastroenterologist determined that he had pre-mature digestion and severe reflux. He gave us a prescription for ranitidine (Zantac) and told us to give Sam a laxative daily. This worked for a few months, until the reflux worsened, and the doc-tor gave us lansoprazole (Prevacid).

The Prevacid worked, and Sam would stay on them well past his first birthday.

The vomiting was under control, he no longer seemed to be in pain after eating, and the constipation had gone away. Every four months, we would go see the gastroenterologist to adjust Sam's meds, if necessary, and make sure there were no other issues.

Aside from this specialist, the only other specialist Sam was seeing anymore was Paladin, the retinologist who did his eye sur-gery in the NICU. Sam had to have his eyes checked every three months to watch how they were healing, and to look for signs that the surgery didn't work.

Each exam was just like the one in the NICU and terrible to

watch, but the results were always good and encouraging. Paladin was confident that Sam's eyesight was intact and he would only have some nearsightedness to contend with in the future.

Nearsightedness was a lot better than near blindness.

With just a few specialists to see, there were few excuses to leave the house. Those many months of RSV season dragged on and on, and my isolation and cabin fever grew. I was still on leave from my job, and the higher-ups were asking me almost daily when I would return to work. I knew I could not go back until RSV season was over, as there was no way I could leave Sam at a day care or nanny share.

More than that, I wasn't sure I was mentally ready to go back.

I had a hard time envisioning being back at my desk, creating marketing materials for the latest technology, after what I had been through. My old life and profession seemed shallow and soulless. My life and priorities had changed so much since Sam was born.

But it was more than that.

I was a total emotional wreck.

I had gone through hell—and come out the other side . . . almost. The trauma of what I had been through was profound, and my internalization of it was deep. Buried in me was pain, suffering, fear, anxiety, and so much more. I found myself crying for no reason and without provocation. I broke out in cold sweats when I heard a beeping sound that was similar to the machines Sam was on in the hospital. Certain soaps made my stomach turn, as their scent transported me back to the NICU.

The thought of going back to my old job added to this emotional stress. Not only would I be walking back into a high-stress job, but I would be doing it at a place that filled me with anxiety. I never wanted to reenter the bathroom stall where I had miscarried one of the twins. I was afraid to see my coworkers, for fear that they would expect me to be the same person I was before Sam's birth, which I knew I wasn't.

Then, in mid-April, my company took the decision out of my hands. They finally ran out of patience and told me it was time to come back. I had been out for almost seven months.

I was angry that they'd given me this ultimatum with just a few weeks left in RSV season. But it wasn't just the danger of RSV that was keeping me from leaving Sam with a nanny. After all we had been through and all the time we had been separated, there was no way in hell I was ready to be separated from him again.

"Peter. I don't see myself returning to work."

He paused. "Do you mean now or ever?"

"I don't know about ever, but I can't go back now."

"What does that mean?"

"I want to resign. I want to be home with Sam and Irene. Maybe I can find some freelance work or something."

"Can we afford for you to leave your job?"

"Honestly, I don't know. But mentally, I can't afford to go back."

Peter agreed and I gave my notice. Just as I had been thrown into the world of the preemie parent, I was now thrown into the world of the stay-at-home mom.

Having the weight of leaving my job lifted was a huge relief, but the continued isolation that came with it fed my anxiety and stress.

By July, I was a bit of a ticking time bomb of emotions.

Then my mom had triple bypass surgery, and the emotional shit hit the fan for me.

I went to see her in the recovery room after her surgery. There she was, lying still, on a ventilator, tubes coming out of her from every possible place. The sounds of the room and the presence of the monitor showing her respiratory rate, oxygenation levels, heart rate, and blood pressure immediately transported me back to the NICU—and not in a good way. I couldn't keep the tears back. I could taste bile rising in my throat and felt my heartbeat quicken.

My mom's nurse noticed the color drain from my face.

"She's going to be OK, honey. She is doing really well," the nurse said, assuming I was worried about my mom.

I did not correct her. It seemed easier to let her believe it was worry than to explain that all the equipment and noise were taking me back to a place I didn't want to be. I gave my mom a kiss and left as soon as I could.

I found a quiet spot in the hallway outside the ICU, sat down on the floor, put my head between my knees, and focused on my breathing. It didn't take too long before I was able to get the panic back under control.

I didn't tell anyone what had happened or why it had happened. Talking about it seemed to make it more real than I was ready to admit. Instead, I pushed all that trauma and fear back down and tried to move forward.

About two weeks later, it happened again. This time, I was in the recovery room after having cortisone injections in my back to relieve pain from a previous back injury. The nurse was wheeling me out of the procedure room and into the recovery area. I was lying flat on my back on the hospital bed when one of the nurses pushed the button to sit me up. Just like last time, I felt the bile start to rise and my heart started to pound. I had not been in a hospital bed lying like that since I was first admitted to the hospital and put into Trendelenburg for six days. I was back in the delivery room just in time to reexperience the overwhelming trauma of giving birth to a micro-preemie.

Again, I hid my distress from the people around me. Somehow the nurses didn't notice the tears streaming down my face.

"Are you in pain?" the recovery room nurse asked me.

I nodded.

"Would you like something to help ease the pain?"

I nodded.

Right about the time I was really starting to panic, the nurse arrived with an anti-inflammatory shot and a painkiller. The drugs immediately took the edge off, and the painkiller kept me numb for the rest of the day.

It wasn't until I talked with my therapist that I fully understood what was going on with me. She diagnosed me with post-traumatic stress disorder (PTSD) and informed me that this was something many preemie parents suffer from—often silently.

I was shocked to hear the diagnosis. In my mind, PTSD was associated with the trauma of war. It never even occurred to me that the trauma of Sam's birth could be a triggering event. I had been suffering in silence for months. I knew things made me feel worse, but I didn't understand that they were triggering a PTSD response. Having my therapist put into words what was happening to me was really helpful.

I still find myself struggling with PTSD. The smell of hospital soap makes my stomach churn. Pregnant women make me angry—especially when I hear them complaining about how tired they are of being pregnant. Old pictures of Sam in the NICU can stop me in my tracks and keep me stopped for hours.

I am hopeful that this will get better in time; however, I know it is something I will struggle with for many years, if not the rest of my life. I think of it as one last gift from the NICU.

Chapter 52

One day, the calendar turned from April 30 to May 1. That simple event meant there could be an end to my isolation. The threat of RSV was over, and Sam and I were allowed out into the world.

This was a big deal. I had been trapped inside a hospital or my house since September 10—the day I first entered the hospital. That is a long time to be isolated.

There were not many people who understood what a big deal this was, except for my NICU-mate, Elisa. Her imprisonment had been longer than mine, as hers had started in the middle of the summer.

We had made a plan. On May 1, we would meet at the most crowded coffeehouse we could find and sit there with our babies uncovered for all the world to see and sneeze on.

OK—not the last part.

I arrived before Elisa and settled in at a table right in the middle of the café. I placed Sam's car seat on a chair and flung the blanket off.

I smiled.

Nobody noticed.

Moments later, the door opened, and in walked Elisa with a

smile from ear to ear. Bennett was in his car seat, no blanket covering him and protecting him from the world outside.

We both were crying.

"Freedom!" Elisa said as she sat down.

"I feel like such a rebel. Look at Sam. Indoors. With people."

We hugged.

The boys slept through the entire event.

That day was the start of a whole new world opening up for not just me and Sam but our family unit as a whole. With RSV over, we resumed some of our favorite family traditions: Saturday breakfast out, friends over for dinner, hanging with friends at their houses, and visiting our favorite local bookstore, A Great Good Place for Books.

The lifting of the isolation restriction also allowed Sam and me to finally film the TV ad we had been asked to make for the hospital. About two months after we were released, I had received a call from the advertising agency working with Alta Bates hospital. The blog that I had been writing reached the head of the hospital marketing department, and they were interested in featuring our story in one of their TV spots. Flattered, and excited for a way to give back to the hospital that had saved my son's life, I told them of course we would do it—but they would have to wait until the end of RSV season.

They were more than happy to wait. They were eager to feature a healthy and adorable baby in one of their ads.

Now that it was May, the process of making the commercial began. Suddenly I had contact with a number of adults in the real world. I got to be part of the other side of video production. One part of my professional career was working on the production side of videos and commercials. Now I was the talent in front of the camera.

When the shoot day finally came, I managed to get through over six hours of filming, telling and retelling my story without shedding a tear. Before we wrapped, the director asked me one last question: "If you were to think of this ad as a thank-you note to the hospital staff, what would you want to say?"

It was the money question. Unable to hold back the tears, I wept as I delivered a marketing executive's dream line.

The commercial began running over the summer. By Sam's first birthday, I was getting tired of seeing myself in HD, though I was flattered to have been asked to represent the NICU.

Then Misty, our social worker from the NICU, called to tell me a story about another family that had seen our TV spot. They lived over a hundred miles from the hospital when the mom went into labor at twenty-three weeks into her pregnancy. Her local hospital told her there was nothing they could do for her or her baby, and that she could wait to deliver in the hospital or at home.

Her husband had seen our ad and told his wife to pack a bag, because they were coming to Alta Bates. He figured if Alta Bates could help me, maybe Alta Bates could help them.

This couple drove one hundred miles, delivered their baby a few days later, and after a few months went home with their beautiful and thriving baby.

I was overjoyed to learn that just by telling Sam's story, we'd given hope to this couple, who'd done what they had to do to give their baby a chance. It propelled me to find a way to share Sam's story further. The idea that I could help parents in a similar situation have faith and confidence that their child could survive was empowering. I wanted to turn my trauma and story into something that would inspire people.

Chapter 53

In the weeks leading up to Sam's first birthday, I began having mild anxiety attacks, which got worse and worse the closer we got to Sam's big day, September 16. It felt so odd to be this sad approaching such a huge milestone, one that a few doctors told us we would never see. And still, each day made me more and more emotional. I cried easily. I got mad easily. I found myself reflecting a lot on everything we as a family had been through.

And we had been through the ringer.

With five days until Sam's birthday, I started to dread the huge celebration I had planned. I wasn't sure I had the strength to get through it. I thought about calling the whole thing off but knew I would regret that decision later. Sam's birthday wasn't just a celebration of his life; it was a celebration of everyone that had helped us make it to that milestone.

On the morning of Sam's birthday, I woke up crying. I am not sure if it was relief that I had finally made it to that day, or terror that I would not survive the day without a meltdown.

Peter had taken the day off to spend with all of us. After getting yelled at, often for no reason, in the days leading up to Sam's birthday, I think he took the day off to watch over me.

We had decided to bring Sam back to the NICU for a victory

tour. It seemed fitting that he should be there one year after his first entry into the unit. Besides, I wanted to see the doctors and nurses who had saved his life and show him off a little.

After putting together a giant gift basket of snacks and treats for the staff, we took the elevator up to the third floor of the hospital and walked down the long hallway to the NICU. Allison and Sonia spotted us before we made it to the door. By the time we entered the unit, word was out that Sam was there. Person after person came up to greet us and hug Sam.

"Look at how big he is!" Teresa cheered as she plucked Sam out of my arms. "He's all mine. You two wash your hands and come find us," she said as she took off with Sam to parade him around the NICU.

By the time our hands were NICU clean, Sam was in the back, doing rounds with Teresa and charming current NICU parents. Just as other children had been paraded around to me, Sam was now the baby bringing hope to current NICU families.

After posing for a few key pictures with Nurse Laura in front of Sam's old room, we headed out to the park for a day of play with Sam.

Once school was over, we picked up Irene and met my parents and family friends who were visiting from Chile at Fentons Creamery for the big celebration. I had held it together most of the day—better than I thought I could.

I kept smiling all through dinner. And then the waitress placed a big bowl of ice cream with a candle in front of Sam and shouted at the top of her lungs: "May I have your attention? We are celebrating a very special birthday today. Today, Sam is turning one!"

I felt like screaming, "You're damn fucking right this is a big birthday!"

And then it happened. The tears started to fall.

Then I began sobbing—uncontrollably sobbing.

People near us were looking at me like I was crazy. Perhaps I was. But there was something about this room full of people happily singing to Sam, blissfully unaware that he wasn't supposed to be there.

He wasn't supposed to survive. He'd had a less than 20 percent chance of living through birth, let alone making it to his first birthday with no major medical issues.

So here, in the middle of Fentons, with happy people all around me, I wept.

I cried for all Sam had endured. All I had lost. All Irene had suffered. All the distance that had entered my marriage. All my parents had sacrificed to support us.

I let it all out.

I wept with each spoonful of ice cream I ate (you are never too upset to eat ice cream).

I wept the whole way home.

I wept as I nursed Sam to sleep.

Once he was down, I finally stopped weeping and I wrote him this letter:

Dear Sam:

It was on this day one year ago that you entered our lives. You were . . . shall we say . . . early. Really, really early. We were not expecting to meet you until January 4, but you just had other plans. The six days prior to your arrival were hard and scary. The ninety-five days you stayed in the hospital after you were born were some of the hardest days of my life. But one year ago, at 6:35 p.m., the most magical thing happened. All one pound, twelve ounces of you changed the course of your mommy's life forever.

You may not realize what a different person I was before you, my sweet boy, and I am glad you won't. The person

I am now is so much better than I ever imagined I could be. Don't let this all go to your head. You are still grounded until you are at least sixteen. I mean, you did put me through hell! But you also changed me for the better.

Because of you, I have learned so much about myself, my friends and family, and the resilience of you.

First, I learned that there is nothing the world can throw at me that I cannot handle. Having a baby born so early is terrifying. You were so small and fragile—and for at least that first month, each hour was a miracle that you were still with us. In those darkest of days, I was there. I was there with you, day in and day out. Holding you, nourishing you, willing you to grow. It didn't matter how hard it was, I was there. If you had to suffer through it, I was going to be there with you. I never thought I was that strong, but I learned from you that strength is there when you need it.

And I needed it. You would not believe the community of people we had around us—supporting us, feeding us, listening to us, thinking good thoughts for us. You had a real fan club—many of whom will be there tomorrow to celebrate your birthday. This amazing community is how I managed to get through each and every day. Some of these people I have known my whole life, some of them I only know because of you, and some of them I have never even met. You are so loved, my little man—and I do not mean just by me.

The biggest thing I learned in this last year is that some superheroes wear onesies. You may not believe this, but in my eyes, you will always be a superhero. Not everyone can be born at such a young age and do nothing but thrive. Yes—there was the whole "scare the crap out of me" heart issue that was repaired way back when . . . but overall, you

*have done nothing but defy the odds. You are amazing—
and there is nothing you will not be able to do in your life.*

*So, after shedding a few tears this evening as we sang
"Happy Birthday" to you tonight in Fentons, I now sit
here in awe of all that you were and are. You have forever
changed me, my son, and I will love you more than I will
ever be able to express.*

*Happy Birthday, Sam—may each year prove over and
over again why you are the super preemie.*

Love,

Your Mommy

Acknowledgments

This book has been a labor of love for the past seven years. I could not have started it, edited it, or finished it without the love and support from my friends, family, and friends that are family.

My amazing daughter, Irene. You made it possible for me to be the mom that Sam needs me to be. I know you have had to deal with more than most kids ever have to deal with, and it has been with great pride that I have watched you navigate becoming Sam's sister and all that entails with grace, humor, and love. You are my rock. And I love you more than you could ever love me. We win.

My parents have been there for me in ways I didn't think possible. When Sam was in the NICU my parents were there with me every day. I do not mean in spirit. I mean literally. Every day one or both of them would be by my side in the NICU. Keeping me company, helping with Sam, and generally holding me up. Since I have become a single mom, my parents have stepped in to help with whatever I need help with. My dad takes his role as Yayo very seriously and has never once let me down. My mom read every draft of this book, editing and correcting like a pro. It was her mission to remove every passive voice sentence, and I am hopeful that we got them all! After her last read, she begged me to get it published so she would not have to read another draft. It breaks my heart that she will never see this book in print.

This book would not have been started had it not been for the relentless encouragement from Kathleen Caldwell, owner of the wonderful bookstore A Great Good Place for Books in Oakland, California. Her bookstore was a refuge for Irene when Sam was born. She became Irene's friend first and mine second. Thank you, Kathleen. You were right.

Gayle Brandise's help and guidance on the drafts of my book were invaluable. She helped push me to take the story further than I thought I would be comfortable doing. I would not be able to call myself a published author without her help.

I would be remiss if I didn't thank the She Writes Press team for taking a chance on me. I especially want to thank Krissa Lagos for encouraging me to make difficult edits and revisions to the book that made it so much better.

When you are in the NICU, all you can hope for is to walk away with a healthy child. I got that and so much more. A friendship formed in the trenches creates a bond like that of soldiers in a foxhole. I was blessed to meet Elisa my first week in the NICU with Sam. Her friendship, shoulder, and unparalleled texting skills have gotten me through so much. I am lucky to have walked away with a souvenir like her. And not just me—the bond and friendship between Sam and Bennett is almost worth a second book!

I am lucky to have a network of friends who encouraged me, pushed me, edited me, and lifted me up—through everything. These friends have been there for it all: childhood, college, marriage, pregnancy, becoming a mom, pregnancy loss, Sam's birth, divorce, and just everyday life. Thank you, Stephanie, Joan, Christain, Stephanie aka Steponme, Lisa, Nadine, Desiree, and Helen for being part of my life.

Thank you will never be enough for the staff of Alta Bates hospital. They did so much more than save Sam's life—they propped me up so that I could be the mom Sam needed me to be. From the nurses in Labor & Delivery to the entire staff of the NICU, you are the most amazing group of people I have ever had the pleasure of knowing. You are all my heroes, and each of you holds a special place in my heart. I would call everyone out by name, but then I would forget someone, and the guilt would kill me. Instead, I will just give Laura Rutherford the shout-out she deserves. Seriously—you kept me sane day in and day out. Your bluntness, sense of humor, and care were my everything for ninety-five days.

And lastly, a huge thank-you to all those that helped with the funding: Lisa Baskin Wright, Doug and Terry Young, Steve and Mary Jane Lowenthal, Jon and Connie Hartung, Steve Bileca and Angela Alonso, Rose Chinguila, Donna and Ralph Briskin, Kathy Cooper, Jill Stevens, Desiree Headberg, Amy Kaplan, Judy Todd, Dave and Debbie Ballati, Clare Rubin, Christain Pitts, Melissa Fully and Steven Rosenberg, Beryl Sallinger Schmitt, Katie Martin, Danny and Susan Shaw (twice!), Linda and Steve Goldfarb, Adela Penner, Jim Haydel, Mike and Nancy Finn, Jen Wolosin, Clay and Kim Clement, Mick and Kris Diede, Jeannie Pfaelzer, Karen Mazur, Kathleen Caldwell, Josh and Gwen Hebert, Joanne Unger, Margaret Alper, Andreina Febres, Carina Hale, Elisa and Bennett, Helen Syreggelas, Ken and Betty Gibbs, Janice Baker Kinney, Lise Melin and Dave Berg, Joan Allen, Elliot Regenstein, Eric Lombardi, Michele Metz, and Martha and Dick Yoshizaki.

About the Author

Photo credit: Gani Piñero

Melissa Harris is a single mother of two children living in Oakland, California, where she was raised. She was on the fast track to being a partner in a mid-size ad agency when she gave birth to her second child, Sam, and the trajectory of her life changed. Melissa is now a work-from-home account manager for two virtual creative agencies in the Bay Area. In her free time, she drives her kids from activities to appointments to playdates, volunteers at the neonatal intensive care unit at Alta Bates hospital where Sam was born, and helps her congresswoman fight for better health care for all Americans.

SELECTED TITLES FROM SHE WRITES PRESS

She Writes Press is an independent publishing company
founded to serve women writers everywhere.
Visit us at www.shewritespress.com.

Expecting Sunshine: A Journey of Grief, Healing, and Pregnancy after Loss by Alexis Marie Chute. $16.95, 978-1-63152-174-4. A mother's inspiring story of surviving pregnancy following the death of one of her children at birth.

The Doctor and The Stork: A Memoir of Modern Medical Babymaking by K.K. Goldberg. $16.95, 978-1-63152-830-9. A mother's compelling story of her post-IVF, high-risk pregnancy with twins—the very definition of a modern medical babymaking experience.

Three Minus One: Parents' Stories of Love & Loss edited by Sean Hanish and Brooke Warner. $17.95, 978-1-938314-80-3. A collection of stories and artwork by parents who have suffered child loss that offers insight into this unique and devastating experience.

Second Chance: A Mother's Quest for a Natural Birth after a Cesarean by Thais Derich. $16.95, 978-1-63152-218-5. Traumatized by an unwanted cesarean, Derich begins the long journey toward learning to trust herself so she can go against societal norms and give birth to her second child the way she wants: naturally, and at home.

Falling Together: How to Find Balance, Joy, and Meaningful Change When Your Life Seems to be Falling Apart by Donna Cardillo. $16.95, 978-1-63152-077-8. A funny, big-hearted self-help memoir that tackles divorce, caregiving, burnout, major illness, fears, and low self-esteem—and explores the renewal that comes when we are able to meet these challenges with courage.

Green Nails and Other Acts of Rebellion: Life After Loss by Elaine Soloway. $16.95, 978-1-63152-919-1. An honest, often humorous account of the joys and pains of caregiving for a loved one with a debilitating illness.